LILLIAN TOO'S
168 Ways to Harness Your
Lucky Numbers
for Wealth, Success,
and Happiness

LILLIAN TOO'S
168 Ways to Harness Your
Lucky Numbers
for Wealth, Success, and Happiness

CICO BOOKS
LONDON NEW YORK

Published in 2010 by CICO Books
An imprint of Ryland Peters & Small Ltd
20–21 Jockey's Fields   519 Broadway, 5th Floor
London WC1R 4BW   New York, NY 10012

www.cicobooks.com

10 9 8 7 6 5 4 3 2 1

ISBN: 978 1 907030 09 3

Printed in China

Editor: Robin Gurdon
Designer: Jerry Goldie

Contents

Introduction

Numbers are at the center of our lives, giving meaning to the birth charts, astrology life maps, and flying star charts at the heart of our personal feng shui. They are the components within these charts that provide clues to how the cosmic vibrations in our living environments interact with our inner vibrations. Numbers—and the way they combine with each other—reveal influences that have a direct impact on the kind of people we eventually become.

The numbers in astrology and feng shui charts reveal a great deal about our attitudes, our luck, our wellbeing, our energy level at different times of our lives, and, most significantly, they offer clues to the options in our lives, showing how the various possibilities of our destiny might unfold. They also give rise to numerology, the practice of reading and acting on the meanings of numbers as well as their sums and combinations. The sum of the numbers associated with our birth date, for instance, tells us a great deal about our aptitudes and character tendencies.

The numbers of your birth and name

If you want to know more about yourself you can use your birth date to discover your Birth Number, to gain an insight into the kind of person you are. It is an excellent gauge of your strengths and weaknesses, acting as an introduction to your personality, your outward perceptions and attitudes as well as the influences that find resonance with your character.

Similarly, the sum of numbers derived from the syllables or letters of your name—your Name Number—also offers clues to your personality. Using numbers in this way also reveals the direction of your life destiny and the nature of its peaks and troughs, addressing your luck more intensely than your personality. As a result many people tend to examine this number in greater depth.

In Asia, many cultures count the number of letters that make up their name in order to arrive at a suitably lucky number that will affect them through their life. The Chinese and Japanese derive this number from the number of strokes used to write their name, the Hindus use the number of syllables to count out their lucky name, while those who use the Western alphabet can exchange numbers for the letters. In many countries of Asia, people have been known to change their name, and therefore their Name Number, should they be convinced their life is unlucky.

When you study the meanings associated with your Birth and Name Numbers, you will get a very good feel about your character tendencies, how you respond to others and to the events in your life. These numbers also offer indications of the things that motivate you the most—what makes you tick and what gets you excited, and hence by extension also what aspirations you have.

Knowing how to use the numbers that are significant in your life will help you to determine the best dates and times for making important decisions, or for changing directions in your life. You can also use them to help you decide on transformational moves and activities that have a direct bearing on your happiness and satisfaction levels. Thus, for instance, you can use them to calculate the suitability of specific job offers, potential life partners, change of homes, as well as some major step you are thinking of taking that may be life changing for you.

This book provides the guidelines to getting answers to these and other dilemmas and thus will assist you to improve your life immensely.

Numbers in feng shui

Numbers also feature strongly in the practice of time-dimension feng shui. This aspect of feng shui is an important core practice of many masters of the ancient science of space enhancement. For them the passage of time is given incredible prominence because the luck of buildings and homes is directly impacted by it.

Using special formulas collectively known as the flying star principles of feng shui, a three-by-three sector grid of numbers is drawn up to track the change of energies. These numbers change from month to month, from year to year, and from period to period. Each grid of numbers is referred to as a flying star chart, and each is comprised exclusively of numbers that reveal the luck of houses and work places. Think of them as showing the influence of chi energy over time. Although time moves from moment to moment, for the purposes of convenience we can think of it in terms of twenty-year cycles as well as on a yearly and monthly basis. In actual fact, of course, energy changes every second but the minute-to-minute changes are so subtle that it is sufficient to read these charts on a less regular basis.

To understand these influences, you first need to know what each number, from 1 to 9 stands for—each number has multiple attributes that have both overt and hidden meanings, as well as gross and subtle nuances. Alone they exert some influences but when they combine with each other, they give rise to new meanings. To the feng shui master, the numbers and their combinations in the flying star charts reveal the quality of chi energy in any designated environment.

Knowing how to read and interpret these numbers is what enables the feng shui practitioner to make the most of his or her feng shui knowledge. This numerology aspect of feng shui is widely regarded as having the greatest impact on the luck of houses—both good and bad.

The numbers reveal the power of the cosmic chi—both beneficial and harmful—within buildings. There are subtle differences to good and bad luck and the Chinese master practitioners of feng shui recognize not just multiple kinds and levels of good fortune, they also have a whole library of terms to describe different kinds of afflictions, misfortunes, and bad luck that are brought by time changes in chi energies! And all these subtle kinds of good fortune and misfortune can be read from the numbers—what is termed the 81 combinations of numbers.

Numbers as "stars" ... indicators of destiny

In the universal cosmic plan, energy is never static and its essence is denoted by the stars that fly into the living space from moment to moment... The "stars" flying into any designated space are expressed as numbers. In flying star feng shui we recognize several different kinds of stars, such as Period stars, Annual stars, and Monthly stars. In addition, flying star feng shui places great importance on two other stars—the

Water and Mountain stars—found in the chart. These stars and the numbers that signify them are what bring potent wealth luck and amazing relationship luck. They are the key to tracking and unlocking the wealth-bringing energy and relationship-enhancing chi into any space!

The nature and essence of these stars, their locations and how to get them "activated" change over time, especially from one twenty-year period to the next. We are currently living through the Period of 8, which began on February 4th 2004 and ends on the same day in 2024. The number 8 Water and Mountain stars are thus very auspicious, very active, and also very powerful. Hence it is incredibly beneficial for everyone who wants to enjoy wealth luck and relationship luck to use the flying star charts to find out where they both are located in their homes; this is essentially the core of flying star feng shui. Once you discover the location of these two incredibly potent stars, all you need do is to activate them so that wealth luck and relationship luck come streaming into your home, benefiting everyone within.

All Water and Mountain stars must be activated before their exciting promise of great wealth and relationship luck can materialize. Knowing how to locate and activate them is the skill of the good feng shui practitioner. Knowing their meanings is however, only the first step—you also need to know how to get them energized.

Once you have begun to understand how numbers work you can use your knowledge in any context you wish to improve your life. Your Birth and Name Numbers can help you decide when to relocate, when to change jobs, when to buy property or invest, when to marry, and when to travel. Your feng shui numbers will show you how to expand your prosperity luck and improve your relationships and health luck. Today, respect for numbers has long been acknowledged and

many of their secrets have already surfaced onto the world's consciousness. The cosmic vibration of numbers resonates closely with the rhythms of our life.

The Golden Mean
This discovery is, of course, not new. Half a millenium before Christ, the brilliant Greek mathematician Pythagoras introduced numerology onto the Western world's body of mathematical knowledge and his ideas resonate strongly with feng shui experts.

A powerful and significant parallel is what Pythagoras describes as the Golden Mean, which feng shui experts describe as the Magic Ratio. However, the Hindu Vedas and Chinese classical literature on both astrology and feng shui predate Pythagoras and they are more generally regarded as the originators of studies into numbers and their significance to the living, and their yang abodes. From India come the powerful Mandalas of numbers known as Yantras and Sigils; from China the Lo Shu and Ho Tu squares are both significant tools used to interpret feng shui charts. These are potent four-sided figures within which are placed rows of numerals that take on a mysterious significance, with many traditionalists still carrying them as powerful protective amulets and talismans.

Numbers in the modern world
There are thus many different ways to look at numbers and to benefit from them. This book shows the reader 168 powerful ways to understand numbers and use them to maximum benefit. There is definitely a potency to numbers and when you effectively generate their vibrations to resonate in sync with your inner self, they are sure to add new dimensions to your life. The key is to determine which numbers resonate with you, then to engage them so that they open the cosmic channels that bring health, wealth, happiness, and success into your life.

Your life and Name Numbers

Your Birth and Name Numbers—made by converting your date of birth and then the letters of your name into single numbers—are the keystones of your personal number feng shui. Discover how to find these numbers and the insights into your personality and future prospects both can give.

1 Knowing your Birth Number

At birth, you are given a set of numbers that add up to your Birth Number, which influences your direction in life.

Your Birth Number is determined by the sum of all the digits that make up your date of birth. While calculating this number is very simple (see Tip 3), it reveals the potential that you possess with respect to your talents, your affinities, and also the direction you tend to follow throughout your life.

Your Birth Number suggests what will bring you the greatest potential for success, satisfaction, fulfillment, and happiness. It is another way of describing your heart's destiny. Your Birth Number is therefore an important dimension of the sum total of numbers that affect your happiness; it provides clues to the kind of success that makes you feel fulfilled.

Your Birth Number influences your life path

The Birth Number is not so much a foretelling indication as a destiny indication, which helps you to identify the path that makes you feel whole and satisfied with life—which is the major benefit of a numerology reading. Knowing your Birth Number is the beginning of a journey into understanding your true nature. It is by understanding yourself at this level, through this first number you derive, that you can then expand your knowledge and awareness into other more subtle levels and areas of your life. When you have begun to understand the significance of your Birth Number you can then proceed to look at other key numbers and explore how they relate to you.

Your Birth Number is a signpost to success, good health, and opportunity

Your Birth Number is not necessarily your lucky number. But it points the way to the numbers that can and do bring you a variety of luck. Once you know your Birth Number, you can use it to relate to many different ways of attracting success, good health, and all kinds of opportunities—what we term "luck."

But first you really should understand how your Birth Number influences and shapes all your attitudes; how it guides you at a subliminal level along life's path. This translates into your affinities and your natural inclinations—how you naturally gravitate towards certain people; how you prefer to take part in certain kinds of activities rather than others, and how you generally feel at home and more comfortable in certain kinds of environments.

There are many aspects to personality, but the most important is how you relate to people and to situations. This basically sums up your approach to life. You will be amazed at what knowing your Birth Number can unfold for you—and you will be stunned by how accurate the numbers can be as you delve deeper in to the numerology of your persona.

Understanding your Birth Number 2

The numbers 1 to 9

Before your begin to calculate your Birth Number (see Tip 3), please note that we work basically with the nine numbers 1 to 9. All the numbers of your date of birth are systematically reduced to a single digit number between 1 and 9. Each of these single digit numbers offers instant insights into the essence of you, But what we analyze must go beyond just the single Birth Number. Later, after you have familiarized yourself with the meaning of your Birth Number, you can go deeper and look into other numbers that are embedded inside the birth date.

Looking at your Birth Number, Day, and Month Numbers

We look also at how the Birth Number combines with other numbers that are aspects of you. Hence we look at the total birth date and then we also look at the day and month components of your date of birth. In Chinese numerology, as in destiny chart reading, the four pillars of birth—the hour, the day, the month, and the year—are given equal importance. In Chinese numerology, therefore, we also look at how the numbers of these pillars interact with each other, though we do simplify this a little by omitting the hour pillar in our investigation.

We will also examine how the Birth Number interacts with the Name Number—eventually adding the two numbers to derive a further "deeper" number. The idea is to systematically look at all the numbers that make up the total of you. The investigation often reveals some fascinating insights into what affects your success luck, and how you can harness the numbers of your life to bring you the kind of fulfillment that you want.

The numbers 11 and 22

There are two additional numbers that resonate with some special force: 11 and 22. When you are an 11 or 22 person, or when you are married to one or are exceptionally close to one, you will find they exert a powerful influence. Number 11s tend to exude personality and charisma.

Watch out for the numbers 11 and 22—they have extra resonance.

3 Working out your Birth Number

Your Birth Number is simply your day, month, and year of birth added together. But you need to do this in a special way: first reducing the Day Number, Month Number and Year Number to three single digits, and then adding these together. See the examples given below.

How to work it out

Person A

This person was born on January 12, 1975. Their Month, Day, and Year Numbers are 1, 3 and 4, which becomes their Birth Number of 8. How?

January = 1, as the first month of the year; the 12th day is added together to give a single number as 1+2 = 3. The year, 1975 is added together as 1+9+7+5 = 22 (not 19+7+5). Reduce the number 22 by adding it together: 2+2=4. So you now have three digits for the month, day, and year: 1, 3 and 4. Add together 1+3+4, which gives 8.

So this person's Birth Number is 8.

Person B

This individual has the birth date of June 10, 1943:

June = 6, as the sixth month of the year, and the 10th day reduces to 1 (1+0=1). The year adds up as 1+9+4+3= 17; 1+7= 8. So your three digits for the month, day, and year are 6, 1, and 8. Add together 6+1+8 and you get 15; again, reduce this to a single number to arrive at the Birth Number of 6.

Person C

The person has their birthday on April 1,1960:

Their Month Number is 4, as April is the fourth month of the year. Their Day Number stays as it is, as number 1. The year, 1960, is added together as 1+9+6+0, which gives 16. Reduce this to a single number, and you get 7. So the Month, Day, and Year Numbers are 4, 1, and 7 respectively. Add together 4+1+7 and you arrive at 12. Reduce this number again, 1+2 = 3. Therefore, this person's Birth Number is 3.

Person D

This individual has their date of birth as June 3 1944. Their Month, Day, and Year Numbers are 6, 3, and 9. The Month Number of 6 (June is the sixth month) and the Day Number is 3. 1944 is added together as 1+9+4+4 = 18, which is then reduced to 9 (1+8). Add together the Day, the Month, and the Year Numbers of 6, 3, and 9, which gives 6+3+9 = 18. One final calculation reduces 1+8=9. So this person's Birth Number is 9.

The essence of you in a single-digit number   4

Your Birth Number must always be seen as the base number affecting you through life. It reveals the dominant traits of personality and the defining attitudes that shape your behavior and reactions. This number is the essence of you, but although two people may have the same Birth Number, it does not mean they are the same.

Indeed the Birth Number reacts to other numbers and it also combines with other numbers and these create a more subtle view of the self. Thus, while basic traits may be the same, how the Birth Number eventually affects a person's life depends upon other numbers as well.

For instance, two people may tend to be volatile and quick-tempered, yet this same volatility of temperament could bring great good fortune to one and abject misfortune to the other.

Same number, different meaning

Likewise, two people may possess the same skill such as an ability to speak persuasively; however one may also possess the success potential to become a great leader while the other finds the ability unappreciated and unrecognized. Thus reading Birth Number indications should merely be the starting point to understanding the essence of you. For the numbers to work for you, it is a good idea to look further for embedded combinations.

Note that in deriving the Birth Number the individual digits representing the day, month, and year must all be added together to reduce them into a significant single digit number, from 1 through 9. For those of you who get final Birth Numbers of 11 or 22, these are special numbers that need not be reduced but can stand alone as master numbers. So 11 stays as 11 and is not reduced to a 2; while 22 is not reduced to a 4.

Your Birth Number may be combined with other numbers that describe your luck and life path.

5 Number 1 people possess success potential

Number 1 is a white number associated with winning. Everyone with a Birth Number of 1 has a subliminal desire to win that goes very deep; they are naturally competitive: they tend to have in mind an invisible scoreboard to keep track of how they are doing compared to others in the same field as them. This is an underlying trait that they apply to their professional and business life.

Number 1 is a Water element number, so it has great potential to manifest success and money luck. The ambitious streak they are born with makes them dream dreams and harbor great visionary aspirations; luckily they also possess natural leadership qualities, which is the defining factor in their lives. Parents of Number 1s will find them strong-willed and even arrogant; so they are not exactly easy to handle. Because they seem so purposeful in the way they carry themselves, parents usually give in to them. This is their first "conquest," and it marks the way they proceed through their life journey.

Number 1 people are associated with winning and success.

Free spirits soar to success

Number 1 people are free spirits who allow few things to stand in their way; they tend to attain success at a young age, rising to the top of their professions with seemingly little effort. In truth though, Number 1s work extremely hard—they just make things look easy. What drives them is their desire to win, to emerge victorious and be in control. These natural leaders aspire to become CEOs of companies and to leave their mark as political leaders. They tend to be loners, dependant mainly on themselves.

They love being the tall poppy, so it is not surprising that others will take potshots at them. They attract both the positive and the negative results of success, and negative emotions such as envy and jealousy will stalk them. But they are also not short of admirers and have their group of hangers-on who gravitate to them, drawn by their natural take-charge attitude. But they are essentially individuals with independent views.

Natural, youthful success

Power comes easily to the Number 1 person—power and success. Number 1s definitely have the potential to become great leaders. So if you are a Number 1 person and you have ambitions to become your own boss, start your own business, rise up the corporate career ladder—or run for high office—you must go for it... You will become very successful if you do not allow doubts or weak-minded friends and loved ones to hold you back. You may not succeed immediately, but ultimate success is assured.

You should have become someone in a position of authority by the time you reach the age of 30–35, and from then on you will always be heading for some goal or other.

A Number 1 is basically self-motivating with enough self-generated enthusiasm, creativity, and determination to inspire others. For you the only thing that might stand in your way would be poor health or high blood pressure caused by over-anxiety. This is because Number 1s tend to be careless about their wellbeing. In the midst of living their dream, they sometimes forget to stop to enjoy their success or to look after themselves.

Number 2 people work best in pairs 6

Number 2 is quite the opposite of Number 1. Where the former can be an incredibly independent, Number 2 is all about wanting partnership and working best as a twosome. When they have someone to brainstorm with, chat to, and turn to for a second opinion they will be instinctively happier and become more effective. Number 2 people generally do not mind submerging their personality for the greater good of whomever they are in partnership with.

This holds true in love relationships as well as business partnership. It will also apply in a work situation and in fact Number 2 people make loyal subordinates—they are better as supporters than as leaders.

Number 2 people are rarely ambitious for material success, though that is not to say they do not want or appreciate it. They do enjoy their efforts bearing fruit but they are careful not to seek out success at any price. They thus tend to be very clear about the sacrifices they may be called on to make in order to achieve success. Often the price of success may be too high for them. They will weight their priorities simply because for them other things, and other people, may be more important for them.

Number 2 people are very much about friendships, soul mates, and romance. They will invest a great deal of their time trying to please loved ones and they live for the people they care about—often to an extent that others cannot understand.

Number 2 denotes loyalty

Number 2s are usually gentle by nature, possessed of imaginative and supportive dispositions. Their passions find expression in the creative and artistic fields. But no matter how much they may enjoy an activity, for them it will always be the loved one who stays at the top of their list of priorities.

For them, the team they are a part of is usually more important than the self. So those in a relationship tend to be exceptionally loyal, and those who are married will almost always place the family first. Professionally, they tend to stay in the same job once they find something they like. Should they be active in competitive sports they can be counted on to be one hundred percent loyal to the team. Number 2 is inherently faithful and loyal, a great ally to have.

As can be expected, the weak spot of the Number 2 is the tendency for the heart to rule the head. Emotions can prevail above logic and sentimentality will exert a disproportionate influence on all their actions. Most of all, love will rule their life. The most important thing to this person is finding a soul mate. Once there is this special someone to share their life with, they will build their lives around that. So Number 2s, as the number suggests work best as a pair!

Number 2 people will build their lives around friendships and finding a soul mate.

7 Number 3 indicates someone highly individualistic

When your Birth Number is 3 you are highly individualistic, have an opinion about everything, and a tendency to be dogmatic and egoistic. As a result the Number 3 person often comes across as imperious and rather arrogant. Definitely you are ambitious and will automatically assume that your role in life is to be the one in charge, and anyone who does not subscribe easily to this will be viewed as a challenge to you.

Individuality and dominance characterize those with a Birth Number of 3.

Number 3 people will never be satisfied being subordinate. They make bad second-in-commands, no matter what the situation. The most dominant trait of a Number 3 person can be a refusal to acknowledge anyone else as more important.

Discipline and leadership rule for Number 3 people

Number 3 people make authoritarian leaders in highly disciplined situations like the army or a multinational corporation where rules are clearly set out and the chain of command is clear. This is because Number 3 people also go very much by the book. They are excellent in carrying out orders and executing strategy. They are not very creative as leaders but they are comfortable in situations where clear cut rules of engagement have been imposed. Number 3 people will be less successful as entrepreneurs because they are uncomfortable in the less defined world of business. But there is a side to them that resonates with an inner need to express their creative and artistic leanings. Thus while they have a capacity for discipline they also have a love of the performing arts—perhaps because discipline is so closely involved in becoming a master performer,

Hard work brings success

People in the performing arts who are Number 3 people will almost always work the hardest to win the recognition of peers and audience. When given free expression this person can achieve outstanding success but it takes time for this side to blossom.

There is only one big obstacle that all Number 3 people face at some point in their adult lives: the obsession with attaining perfection. When this quest is too dominant, they lose sight of reality. This can cause major relationship problems and stand in the way of their life's fulfillment, perhaps even cost them happiness.

Those who love Number 3s view their individualistic tendencies as eccentricities, or as diva-like behavior and they are forgiving, but those not close to you will prefer not to have you in their lives. Number 3 people can thus be prickly. It is hard for Number 3s to have close friends or confidantes.

Those who succeed may have material gains and live comfortably, but unless they work at softening their harder side, they may be lonely in old age. Those who do not succeed might become bitter with frustration. You must learn to be kinder to yourself and to those around you.

Number 4 people view the world through rose-tinted glasses

8

Number 4 people are emotionally sensitive individuals who tend to see the world through rose-tinted glasses. They are eternal optimists who prefer to see the good side in people so they always interpret things done to them in a positive rather than a negative way. As such, Number 4s are generally happier than most as they do not imagine themselves being wronged, insulted, or snubbed. Their life is usually more simple than most people but they also seem to have an effective recipe for happiness. They will consciously turn away from those who are pessimistic, having an aversion to the dark side of people and events.

Number 4s can be literary geniuses

In terms of talents this group of people has the potential for literary excellence; you can become a best-selling writer, a successful playwright, or carve out a great career in journalism, or even rise to be editor of a newspaper or magazine. You have a genuine and keen interest in people and the events that take place around you so yours is a world view that is quite wide ranging.

Despite this, however, the child within you can be naïve and you stay this way until quite late in life. Happily you will mature and eventually get more savvy—just that you take longer to acknowledge to yourself that there can be a darker side to people's motivations.

Happiness over money

Number 4 people are rarely super ambitious. For them making it big is "nice" but not something they madly crave for; as such Number 4 people allow themselves to be distracted in multiple life directions. They enjoy the good life but take it in

their stride. Number 4 people are also not strongly motivated by money. They are not big on the accumulation of assets. To them happiness does not equate to a big bank balance. It is being able to spend time with a loved one, being able to pursue some passion, or to travel and indulge themselves. The accumulation of wealth comes low in their list of things to do!

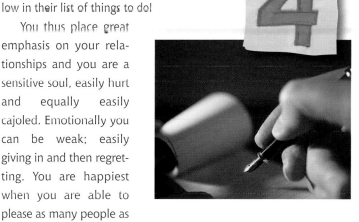

You thus place great emphasis on your relationships and you are a sensitive soul, easily hurt and equally easily cajoled. Emotionally you can be weak; easily giving in and then regretting. You are happiest when you are able to please as many people as possible. Number 4s make great life partners and will find fulfillment doing community or social work. They are great traveling companions as they are sporting and easy to please.

If there is a downside to their do-good attitudes it is that they demand too much of themselves and others; their "kind" intentions can be difficult to stomach to those who get too much of it. So if you are a Number 4 do be aware of your tendency to be just a little too helpful. But if you want to feel happy and fulfilled seek out those who appreciate you, those who identify with your interests. Have the courage to acknowledge what you really want and you will find life opens up and resonates with your interests and inclinations.

Number 4 people often have literary talent, and are romantic in their outlook.

9 Number 5 people are strong types with great determination

Those whose birth date reduces to a Number 5 are freedom-loving, independent souls who are also strong; possessing the potential to become the pillar of their family, of their organization and if they end up as leaders, of their community.

The main characteristic of a Number 5 person is how strong and well-balanced they are; there is determination and a focus in their character and personality that attracts others like them. They will also live their life and do their work in a strong purposeful way so they rarely if ever miss the main chance. Number 5 people are naturally protective of those under their care and also hugely popular with those around them. They are sociable people who can bring optimism, inspiration and excitement to those around them. A major strength they have is the ability to galvanize people into action.

Number 5 people are positive and forward-thinking, determined to succeed.

Efficiency drive

They are enthusiastic about everything they do, being extremely fast in the way they think and react. But their pace of work sets some standards that others find hard to keep up with. Number 5s can be frighteningly efficient but they also have a great instinct—often possessing the ability to smell out good ideas and spotting opportunities. In this sense Number 5s are extremely creative in the way they build their businesses and the way they take risks. What others may see as incredibly impulsive actions will usually have been well thought through.

Number 5s work best when they can showcase their capabilities and it is beneficial for them to attain success in their thirties rather than their twenties because then they have the benefit of some experience behind them. They are great travelers and absorb knowledge extremely well. They learn fast...

Number 5s are great communicators

With experience behind them, Number 5s find high success in the fields of research and communication—as writers, teachers, performers, and even as icons of success. They have amazing charisma and can arrange their lives to inspire others. As long as they do not become self centered—as many of them are prone to do—they can be effective in championing some worthwhile cause. They can be effective catalysts for change!

When Number 5s also have 5 as their Name Number the likelihood of them rising to great heights of achievement is very high. Thus one of the best ways for you to ensure success in whatever you do, and especially if you are in an iconic position hoping to inspire others to your cause, then thinking up a name that reduces to 5 would be an excellent feng shui way to do it!

Number 6 people are blessed with heaven luck   10

listeners and tend to be highly respected by others. If you are a Number 6 person do not be surprised if you find that others tend to want you as their BFF there is something about you many will find attractive and trustworthy.

Fortune favors Number 6

There is also an air of wisdom about the way you carry yourself and respond to situations. People will simply expect you to "know" about spiritual subjects; and indeed, according to many masters of numerology, Number 6 people are what they term "old souls"—who are wise beyond their years and possessed of a compassionate and kind heart. These are people who are spontaneously helpful, nurturing and caring.

Healers, carers, and those in the medical profession often have number 6 as their Birth Number.

Those with Birth Number 6 are people who have an extremely powerful aura around them. It is as if they are blessed by the Gods in the way they attract others to them. They have great charisma and can be extremely magnetic; they instill great love and are often worshipped by those who get close to them.

Number 6 people are blessed with good fortune luck most of their lives. It is likely that many are either born into relatively comfortable backgrounds, or, if they are not, will find their way into a comfortable situation. Number 6 people are born greatly blessed as help always comes to them whenever needed.

They are rarely short of friends and are usually well loved by peers and colleagues. They exude a peaceful and calm demeanor and are a natural magnet for confidences and the secrets of others. This is because they make good

You always make great health professionals—doctors and nurses, counselors, and community aid workers. Whenever you are called on to play the role of care provider, that is when you are the happiest of all. Looking after others seems to be the vocation for you, so throughout your life there will be this subconscious urge to help other people. Should you, as a Number 6 person, ever be called upon to help others in need or to head

a charity drive for the disabled or poor, for example, do accept, even if you do not feel that you possess enough talent or capability to do so. You will surprise yourself, because some kind of divine help will come to assist you.

11 Number 7 people are focused intellectuals

Those whose Birth Number is 7 are very clearly smart and focused people; independent and extremely analytical in the way they think. There is a restlessness about them that makes them want to be always on the move. When they are younger they tend to be quite cheeky but as they mature into adults, Number 7 people will develop into very analytical and also very politically-minded individuals—capable of being quite crafty indeed in the way they deal with their colleagues and peer groups.

Number 7s are global thinkers

Number 7 people think globally. Their minds are like the great big oceans—vast, deep, and far-reaching in the way they think, analyze and make judgments. From a positive perspective this makes them embrace a world view of abundance and the work they do will benefit from how expansively they think. Therefore a Number 7 person running a business or even a country will be quite panoramic in the way they make their decisions.

Nobel prize-winning scientist Stephen Hawking is a Number 7 person, born on January 8, 1942.

Number 7s think beyond their immediate world, often taking a global perspective.

This literally transforms them into magicians, capable of bringing about changes that potentially have a sweeping effect. Their reach gets widened tremendously as a result and all because they intellectualize their decisions in a big, positive way.

There is a great deal of unexpected "out-of-this world" knowledge inside a Number 7 person, knowledge of an instinctive, esoteric nature—and it is beneficial for you to let your imagination flow. This will balance your right-brain thinking. Number 7 people have great intellects, are deep thinkers and possessed of excellent powers of concentration. You must give yourself a chance by being sure to balance and to develop this great mind of yours.

Dealing with sensitivity

If Number 7s are negative they will demonstrate an excessive sensitivity to the words and actions of others, reacting badly to imagined slights, as a result of which their potential for change becomes heavily curtailed—the magic within them unable to find an outlet. If you are Number 7 and feeling frustrated with life, try thinking out of the box—try thinking with a bigger heart and bigger mind—doing so will instantly put you in touch with the powerhouse inside you. Sweep aside all petty thinking and you will be amazed how your life will instantly change!

Remember, however, not to mix up knowledge with intellect. The ability to reason, to create strategies, and to come to meaningful judgments is different from the pure acquisition of knowledge. A Number 7 person has the potential to think deeply and creatively. So for you, getting the knowledge is always easy. It is what you do with the knowledge you acquire that can make you very special! You are sure to be excellent at math, so pursuing work in the sciences is the way to go.

Number 8 people enjoy great abundance luck 12

Those whose Birth Number reduces to 8 possess the potential for acquiring great and amazing abundance, unless they allow themselves to get mired down in complicated life situations that cause their luck to get blocked. So Number 8 people must guard against getting distracted; they must be clear from the start what they want from life. For them there is little room for prevarication because theirs is a life in which distractions come all the time.

Focus brings success!

For Number 8 people, the more focused they are the greater their chances of attaining success and finding fulfilment in what they do. The problem will be that very often they let themselves get distracted by pursuing goals that force them into too many different directions. It is then that their efforts get scattered.

The Number 8 is, however, a "white" number, whose element is Earth. This suggests that hidden within them will be seeds of great abundance and the challenge is only to find the key to unlock this abundance. This means working hard at staying single-minded about the things that they want from life, the lifestyle they want to pursue, and the goals they wish to achieve.

Number 8s like being their own boss

Number 8 people are more comfortable being their own boss and this means being an entrepreneur and having their own business. They are really more comfortable being commercial and making deals than being an executive or administrator. Number 8's line of work is always associated with abundance, with the handling of money, the acquisition of assets, and the merchandising or making of products. Number 8s are also rarely reckless with money so they possess the potential to be successful in the world of commerce and business.

Number 8s are often concerned with making money. Focusing on their goals will also bring material success.

Indeed, Number 8 is very much about wealth and its acquisition. Whether this makes them fulfilled or happy depends on how well-balanced their life is. Number 8s tend to have little interest in matters outside the material aspects of life, and here is where their lack of balance can take its toll.

If there are other key numbers that bring extra dimensions into their world, Number 8's life will be more rounded and balanced.

13 Number 9 people are idealistic and tend to be righteous

Number 9 people are very capable people who have a great sense of duty and a highly developed sense of responsibility. They are idealistic and pride themselves on having high principles. They possess grit, often a strong will, and determination, so Number 9s have the potential to become influential figures in their communities; usually being highly respected and looked up to.

Number 9s think of themselves as honorable people with lofty ideals, so they tend to be rather more judgmental than most in the way that they interact with people. They can be quite unyielding and dogmatic when involved in a managerial situation; they can also be impatient and often will pull rank when caught in any work scenario.

Number 9s can exert amazing influence and achieve great things when they control their tendency to self-righteousness.

Having said this, it is also necessary to point out that the essence of the 9 person is that they often have hidden tendencies toward taking the kind and compassionate route. This reflects their genuine belief in spirituality and the path of ultimate goodness. The only danger is that they become so tunnel vision in their cultivation and championing of the "goodness" within mankind that they can lose sight of the mundane realities of life's imperfections.

As a result, they often allow themselves to get carried away by their sense of right, and then they become righteous. In seeing themselves as selfless individuals they expect similar mindsets from others and when this is not forthcoming, it can lead them to become dangerously bigoted.

Use your charisma to effect

Number 9s are big on causes... They seem to find their vocation in saving the world, in being very green, very environmentally conscious. Some even become preachers and spiritual teachers who, as long as they stay down to earth, can be excellent forces for good.

Number 9 people possess charisma and a power of speech that can transform lives. If you are a 9, as long as you stay balanced and avoid becoming excessively righteous, you have the potential to be amazingly influential in the lives of many people.

Number 11 people have great concentration power

14

Numerologists believe that the number 11 is a master number, which indicates special potential—Number 11s may access a higher spiritual plane than single-digit people. Anyone whose birth-date digits add up ultimately to 11 will possess great intuitive abilities which, if developed, can transform into a psychic force that is very special indeed. The number 11 is as difficult to live with as it is rewarding, however. Sometimes the attributes of the master number 11 can also apply to those born on the 11th day of any of the 12 months; or to those born on January 1, as this is often written as 1.1, or those born in the month of November, the 11th month of the year.

The Number 11 person's psychic abilities can be developed and fine tuned into an ability to project mentally created thoughts into reality. They are people who have a greater than normal ability to use mind power to actualize what they want in their lives. Some people call this magic—those who understand about these things call it a highly developed state of mental concentration. The key for Number 11s therefore is to consciously work at transforming their minds into powerful tools through constant and regular practice.

The positive effect of repetition

When the same number 11 is repeated in the life of a Number 11 person, for instance as address number, telephone numbers, bank account numbers, and so forth, its impact becomes strengthened and then positive luck manifestation becomes a reality in meaningful ways. This leads to situations of great abundance. The luck generated brings either great wealth or some great talent that generates wealth. This, then, is the truly awesome potential of the number 11.

Often, even from a very young age, if you are influenced by the number 11 you will somehow become aware of your special mental capabilities and over time as you grow up, you will use them without realizing that they are special, and that few others possess them.

Number 11s usually excel in their school work, mainly because they will have better concentration than most. As to ambition, however, Number 11s are not the type to be driven, and they do not want or need to succeed at all costs! But there will always be an undercurrent of expectation in the way they react to the world and respond to other people, without them knowing why they feel the way they do.

Number 11 people aware of their significance are instantly at an advantage because simply knowing they possess special concentrative abilities will open new possibilities to them. Once their minds are tuned into the right frequency, they will very quickly begin to understand, and then to develop and harness their special abilities.

As they mature and grow older, 11s become increasingly spiritual in their outlook—not necessarily religious, but definitely spiritual—pursuing studies and research into cultural and esoteric phenomenon. Mystical arts and practices engage their interest and they will be very adventurous and investigative about such matters. Some even make this their life's work.

Many Number 11s possess psychic abilities, and a great talent for concentration.

15 Number 22 people possess the urge to build and create

The Number 22 is similar to the Number 11 but where the 11 focuses on the mental, Number 22 brings forth the power of action, aggressively transforming the creative imagination of the Number 11 into concrete form. Number 22 people have great potential to build on a significant scale. Those who are able to live up to this potential will go on to become extremely powerful and that will be when they realize their fullest potential. To successfully marshal their forces to reach their ultimate potential however, the causes and conditions must come together for them.

Number 22 people can be masters of manifestation— turning their thoughts into reality.

People born with this number need to have their creative talents strengthened, nurtured and given free rein. Anyone having this number will become increasingly aware of the urge to build and create as they mature and grow older. The chance of positive opportunities opening pathways for the fulfilment of the 22 potential becomes stronger if the same number gets repeated within the vicinity and life of the person either as house addresses, car numbers, or telephone numbers.

The number 22 can thus be viewed as some kind of "lucky number." The Number 22 person should closely watch the 22nd of each month so that some kind of empirical guideline is generated for you to see exactly what kind of significant things happen to and for you on this date of each month. After some months you will begin to see a pattern of luck emerging in the days associated with 22 in your life.

Number 22s have a vision related to the field of work within which they find themselves. Most prosper as property and real-estate developers because their urge to build goes beyond merely putting bricks and mortar together. They are "big-picture" people who devote large chunks of time to planning, designing, and creating the pieces of their lives to come successfully together to actualize their visions.

Success through thought

A Number 22 person is as awesome in their mental powers of concentration as a Number 11. What germinates in their head has a better than average chance of taking root and growing into a big plant. What they think about can actually materialize into reality so when you know that you are a Number 22 person it is important to train yourself to think consciously and to choose your thoughts carefully. There is great power in your thought processes.

Many people with the number 22 succeed in amassing some significant wealth. But as you grow older and wiser, you will begin to channel your powers into more meaningful projects that benefit others more than you.

Destiny indications are in your Birth Number 16

We have seen, then, that there are nine single digits and two master numbers—11 and 22—that form the basis of the numerological patterns of a person's life. These numbers must be seen only as starting points in your investigation of how numbers affect and influence your life and your destiny.

The numbers indicate potential and likelihood of the broad areas of life that are associated with you. Destiny describes the kind of life and lifestyle you are likely to lead. So the Birth Number creates the general indications of your life's journey. You will find that your Birth Number provides the basic scenario for you to create and build a life around.

Your Birth Number in combination with other key numbers such as your Name Number, indicates your life path and helps you achieve your potential to maximize your luck.

The three aspects of luck

Please note that as with feng shui luck, there are three aspects of luck when we use numerology to reveal our destinies:

* The luck we are born into
* The luck of our surroundings
* The luck we create for ourselves.

Numerology offers clues about our heaven luck, which reveals the kind of circumstances we are born into. In numerology, aspects of our heaven luck are revealed as derived numbers, and these numbers help us read and get clues about our life's journey, our environmental luck, and also the probability of our attaining the success we want through our own efforts and our responses to situations.

The Birth Number is thus one of the numerical destiny indicators that reveal our tendencies and affinities. But note that these affinities are heavily influenced by other numbers embedded inside the birth date, which create combinations of numbers that give additional clues about our luck.

These numbers are thus better indicators of our destiny than just looking at our surroundings. When the numbers in our life bring good fortune, then even if we are born into disadvantaged circumstances, they can propel us into situations that enable us to fulfil our potential. So take note of what your Birth Number is telling you, then look at other numbers embedded within your date of birth to see how they combine with your Birth Number.

17 Lucky combinations embedded in your Birth Number

Discover the number "specials" in your Birth Number to activate hidden talents.

There are combinations of numbers embedded in your date of birth that bring hidden good fortune. You just need to learn how to detect them, and to activate those combinations that work strongly in your favor. The combinations point to hidden skills and talents that help you realize great success and attainments. Lucky or special combinations in your date of birth are revealed when you reduce your month/day/year of birth into three single digits (which are then further reduced into a final single digit, which is the Birth Number). In many instances, looking at number combinations offers a more detailed numerology reading than looking at the Birth Number alone.

We started with the Birth Number to get an idea of personality types and general affinities; the single-digit Birth Number usually points to destiny and behavior patterns. Now we can go deeper and look at some special combinations that pinpoint the ultimate direction your life will take. These also indicate the consequences of positive as well as negative outcomes.

The presence of the "specials" in your birth date are stand-alone indications of good-fortune potential. Whether or not they get activated and

Combinations of numbers that are indications of good fortune

These examples will help you go back to your Birth Number calculations and find additional number combinations which will offer additional clues to your destiny.

Person A: January 12, 1975 reduces to a Birth Number of 8: 1+ 3 (1+2=3) + 1+9+7+5 = 26, 2+6=8). Note also that the Day Number is 12, which is reduced to a 3, so this person is a strong 8 person whose lucky number can be 12 (8+3=12), the Day Number of his birth date. Note that the 3 derived from this person's Day Number has a powerful connection to the Birth Number of 8, as the 3 and the 8 combines to become a Ho Tu combination of 3/8, which brings some powerful luck as well. (See Ho Tu Numbers, Tips 141–2)

Person B: June 10, 1943 reduces to a Birth Number of 6. Here the Day

Number is 10, which reduces to the number 1. More significantly, however, are the numbers 1, 6, 8 embedded in the birth date. This trinity of numbers are the Day, Month, and Year Numbers respectively that signify the date of birth, with each reduced to a single digit. Together, the numbers 1, 6, 8 create one of the most auspicious combinations of numbers and they bring excellent good fortune to a person, particularly when you know how to activate this combination to fire up your daily life. (See Tips 136–140 for other powerfully auspicious combinations.)

Person C: April 1 1960 reduces to a Birth Number of 3; The Day Number is 1 and with a trinity combination of 1,4,7 representing day, Month and Year, but 1,4,7 is also a three-period combination number that is regarded as very favorable. Here the Birth Number does not combine

in any special way with the Day Number, so the Birth Number becomes more dominant, exerting greater influence on the personality of the person.

Person D: June 3, 1944 reduces to a Birth Number of 9, a Day Number of 3, and the all-powerful three-period combination numbers 3,6,9. This person is thus very much influenced by the number three and will have a special affinity to trinities or in multiples of 3. The trinity combination also brings the potential of extreme good fortune. (Read more opposite about the combination of 3,6,9 as a three period combination number.)

Person E: May 11, 1952 reduces to a Birth Number of 6. The Day Number is 11, which itself is a very special number as you will see later. Anyone born on an 11 day or on an 11 month (November) usually

Combinations with other numbers 18

manifest as real good fortune depends on how you respond to the opportunities and people who come your way and enter your life. But having the potential for success is vastly better than having no potential at all.

Number combinations can be incorporated into numerology readings for you to get a more complete picture of all the possibilities and potential that lie in store for you. So let us look again at examples of Birth Numbers, some of which were shown in Tip 3, except now we will also take note of the special combinations of numbers that are indications of good fortune.

has the destiny to achieve a high level of attainment irrespective of what he or she does in life. The number 11 is regarded as a master number—it is amongst other things the number of attainment, indicating a workaholic as well as someone with amazing powers of concentration, and also a low tolerance level for boredom. (see also Tips 33 and 35). This particular date of birth also indicates an embedded trinity combination of numbers 2,5,8, which is a three-period combination number that signifies extreme good fortune. This trinity of numbers are the day, month, and year respectively that signify the date of birth, with each reduced to a single digit. Together the numbers 2,5,8 create the trinity of earth numbers, which blend amazingly well with the Birth Number of 6. This is because the number 6 is a heaven number and with heaven and earth present in your birth date number, there is created within your life the all-powerful trinity of tien ti ren—or earth, heaven, and mankind.

Significant numbers are embedded in your Birth Number—as two- and three-number combinations—that can offer very positive indications of good luck. So it is important to know what these number combinations are. Here are the two-digit combinations to look out for:

Your Birth Number can reveal special combinations.

* **The sum of ten**. These are 1 and 9, 2 and 8, 3 and 7, 4 and 6, and 5 and 5. They all add up to 10 and the sum of ten reduces itself to the master winning number 1, which is itself the number of success. When the sum of ten is present in your birth date, it is a very auspicious indication and thus very useful to activate.

How? Do this by becoming aware of the appearance of sum of-ten-numbers each time you encounter them—these are telling you that anything associated with the sum of ten reflected in your Birth Number combinations will be bringing you luck. This can be the time, your telephone number, dates, and so forth.

* **The Ho Tu combinations of good fortune**, which are 1 and 6, 2 and 7, 3 and 8, and 4 and 9. These bring specific types of good fortune.

Three-digit combinations to look out for in your Birth Number include:

* **The Lo Shu combinations** of 147, 258 and 369—these are considered to be very special "numbers." These combinations bring amazing good fortune that tends to be long lasting and, better yet, tends to spill over to the next generation—those possessing this combination of numbers often propel their children to great heights of achievement as well. This means you have great mentoring power. Your children will tend to honor and respect you.

* **The combination of the three white stars, 168.** When your date of birth possesses these three numbers embedded within it, the indication is one of great good fortune indeed. The numbers 1, 6, and 8 are bringers of success luck. When you activate them by repeating these numbers in your life, for example as your car registration number, in your home or office address and so forth, it brings success to the forefront of your consciousness. These are excellent ways of activating lucky numbers that have a special resonance with your life and luck energy.

19 Converting your name into a number

Your Name Number describes the kind of work that taps directly into your natural abilities and talents. It helps you choose your life's direction, and gives you the confidence to live the kind of life you want. Your designated career path and the kind of work that interests you is often influenced by and resonates with the name you are known by—this is what leads to a sense of happiness and satisfaction. So there are numerical implications in your name, which is why it's very important.

Choosing the name that means most to you

Your Name Number describes talents at your disposal in this lifetime and is derived from the letters that make up your name. Most of us have different names—those we are born with, nicknames, special names known only by our loved ones, and married names. If you have only one name that everyone knows you by and this is also your birth name, then it becomes a very dominant Name Number and the attributes associated with that number will very likely describe you and your life's destiny very accurately indeed.

If, on the other hand, you have different names by which you are known in the different circles of your life, then it is likely that more than one number fits you. Those with two or more Name Numbers will find that the effect of each of the numbers then gets diluted... and that you

actually present different personality patterns when with different groups of friends. For instance, your nickname known to a close circle will be different from a corporate name by which you may be known. This is a judgment call for you, and only you will know which name has greater meaning for you, or with which part of your life each of your names resonates most.

Remember that if the name on your birth certificate is not a name you use at all, then that is not the name to use to calculate your Name Number. If you use your birth name but you spell it differently as in a nickname then you should use the altered spelling to derive your Name Number.

Unlocking your career potential

Your Name Number shows you what you really are capable of achieving. So, from being just good at something, you can become great at it; it's the difference between being ordinary and being a star! When you engage in doing something that resonates with your Name Number, it means that the energy you create doing your work will blend beautifully with the energy associated with your name... it is an uncanny connection that takes place here, and it engages energy at the invisible cosmic level.

How to calculate your Name Number

To calculate your Name Number, simply convert the letters of your name into numbers according to the conversion table and then add up all the numbers until they get reduced to a

A	B	C	D	E	F	G	H	I	J	K	L	M	N	O	P	Q	R	S	T	U	V	W	X	Y	Z
1	2	3	4	5	6	7	8	9	1	2	3	4	5	6	7	8	9	1	2	3	4	5	6	7	8

single digit from 1 to 9, or to the two special numbers 11 and 22—these special numbers are indicative of special vocations, and as with the Birth Number we also respect the special status of these two numbers.

The Name Number reveals your true vocation and it helps you to identify what kind of direction will enable you to reap the seeds of greatness that lie within you. Read what each of the numbers is telling you about your true potential and think this through carefully. It does not matter what kind of work you are currently engaged in. Also note that sometimes unknowingly you may change the name you are known by—as in when you get a divorce, change life situations, and so forth... Some people also change their name for no reason other than to get a "luckier" number!

So many people change direction half way through their life that it should really not surprise anyone reading this book that this is something that can happen to you too. For me I changed my profession several times before I finally found my true calling.

My Name Number

Let me share my Name Number with you. It is an uncanny fact, but for me my two Name Numbers are both 11. When I was at business school in Harvard, I was known by my Chinese name, Kim, before I later started using my married name, Lillian Too, Both times my Name Number added up to 11, which really resonated with my destiny, bringing me exactly the kind of luck that I needed at those moments of my life!

The word Kim means gold which is Metal, but Metal destroys Wood, which is my self-element, whereas the name Lillian means a flower and flower is Wood, which strengthens my Wood element! So when you add the feng shui five elements and four pillars readings to your name analysis you can see how numerology can add an incredible extra dimension to your luck. The name Lillian Too has many lucky features, so it basically created the luck for me to be doing what I am now doing in my life. For me the surprise was not

L	I	L	L	I	A	N	T	O	O	= 47 (4+7)
3	9	3	3	9	1	5	2	6	6	= 11

P	K	I	M	L	I	M	= 38 (3+8)
7	2	9	4	3	9	4	= 11

Use the top grid to calculate your Name Numbers, using all the names you are known by.

that I changed directions from being a corporate person involved in high-finance mergers and acquisitions work but that I am doing something so incredibly different from what I was doing 30 years ago... The power of my Name Number is shown because I am so incredibly happy doing what I am currently doing—which is to be a writer sharing information about a subject as fascinating as feng shui.

As a Number 11 person my true calling is to be a conduit of spiritual and esoteric information. As I am currently so involved with researching, compiling, and sharing knowledge of the esoteric traditions of a spiritual and feng shui nature, I know that it is because I am living out my number 11 so completely and thoroughly.

This number is further strengthened by the fact that my birthday is 11 and the house I have lived in for over 30 years is number 11. This is more than a coincidence, of course, as we did not choose this house based on its number ... but I can tell you that this house has brought us amazing harmony and good fortune.

In the following pages are the interpretations for your Name Number. Read each section carefully to see what your Name Number reveals for you about your latent talents or abilities. Think through what can be explored or developed to bring you greater fulfilment, irrespective of at what stage of life you are currently.

The interpretations complement the meanings of the Birth Numbers and when both Birth and Name Numbers are the same it strengthens the effect of that number in your life. Perhaps then it can be considered to be your lucky number!

20 Name Numbers 1 and 2

Name Number 1:
Leaders

With Name Number 1, you have every chance of emerging as a leader in whatever you do in life—it is as the person in charge that you will reach your highest potential. This is the best way for you to showcase all your strengths and your ability to make good judgments. Your talents include an uncanny ability to think outside the box; to be original in your approach to finding solutions; to embrace creativity, and best of all to be open-minded in your management style. You are also a very secure and confident person, so you can really bring out the best in others. It is as a leader that you can maximize your fullest potential.

Number 1s are natural leaders with good business brains. Number 2s make brilliant salespeople as they love communicating, and are at their best in the company of others.

Socially or professionally, the person whose name leads to number 1 is the person that has the best chance of making things happen. They make great political leaders and business entrepreneurs. If you work under someone you do not respect, you are sure to feel frustrated, and if you work under an idiot it will feel like torture!

You have to get out!

Name Number 2:
Communicators

You always express yourself best by relating to others. Name Number 2s are those who make the ultimate communications geniuses, diplomats, managers, fabulous salespeople, and very effective persuaders. Any line of work that requires someone talkative, with that natural gift of the gab, is the perfect job for Name Number 2 people.

Socially, you are very popular and have so many friends and contacts everywhere that your chain of influence will be impressive. But it is an influence that you always exert quietly and authoritatively without too many people knowing—you are able to pull big strings in order to facilitate seemingly impossible tasks.

However you are someone who cannot work or live alone. You are a people person and you are at your best when you ally yourself with another person, probably someone terribly powerful and important. While the other person gets the glory and name you are the one calling the shots, and doing the work!

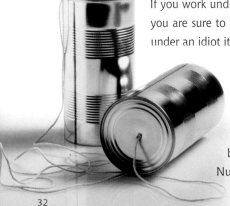

Name Numbers 3 and 4 21

Name Number 3: Performers, artists

When your name reduces to a number 3, it means there are artistic inclinations that are very dominant within you waiting for expression. The potential for you to succeed in a big way exists for you through the arts—such as music, painting, or the performing arts. People like you have the power to lift many others to heights of ecstasy and delight if they can somehow connect with a showcasing of your talent.

So note that with a number 3 Name Number, you will have the potential to become incredibly successful and your work also can offer meaning for many people. Some of you could become very famous and renowned, although there will also be some moments of loneliness; this is because creative geniuses often get lost in a different plane of existence.

For those of you who do not become big successes, it is likely that you will lead a happier, more contented life. As long as there is an outlet for your creative impulses you will have fulfillment.

Name Number 4: Builders, inventors

Those whose name reduces to a Number 4 are people with a hidden impulse and talent to build and to create. In numerology terminology, you would be described as someone who is happiest when creating pockets of space energy.

You possess the scientific and logical mind to bring building projects to completion and this does not just refer to buildings. It also

means that you can create an organization, or bring together a group of people in pursuit of a powerful shared goal. You have awesome organizational abilities lying dormant inside you.

Number 4s have an almost intrinsic understanding of how structure and space are created; but you also have an eye for the visual and an ear for the rhythms of energy wafting through confined living spaces. So your highest potential is to build space that resonates with people, making their lives easier and always more pleasant.

You will make a great property developer, architect, space designer, or building contractor. Those of you involved in doing anything related to these fields of industry are more than likely to find great success. You can also be successful creating other vehicles of communication, such as books, movies, and documentaries.

Name Number 3s are natural creatives, whereas Name Number 4s make great inventors.

22 Name Numbers 5 and 6

Name Number 5: Wisdom teachers

A Name Number 5 person is a person of many talents. They are gurus, teachers, and coaches who impart valuable techniques, knowledge, and attitudes to others—basically all coming together in a lyrical flow of knowledge energy radiating outwards from you. A Number 5 person has a lot to give and share with others, and this is because you are likely to be multi-talented with abilities that take you beyond the scope of ordinary reality. There are hidden gems within you waiting to find fertile ground.

Number 5 people are also very courageous, not afraid to try anything new; you will be adventurous and open minded. Your deepest desires are to test the boundaries of knowledge personally. As you grow older you exude an innate wisdom, the kind that cannot be easily taught and which has little to do with knowledge and instead has a lot to do with understanding the depth and intensity of the human psyche.

You will be a great success working in any aspects of the teaching profession!

People with a Name Number of 5 tend to be natural teachers and gurus.

Name Number 6: Healers

As a Name Number 6 person you will discover that you have an uncanny ability to speak with confidence and authority on subjects related to physical and mental well being. You will have a highly developed sense of inner and outer balance and you instinctively seek perfect balance and equilibrium each time.

Number 6 people will find, as they grow older with each passing year, that they are indeed exceptional individuals. They will become increasingly aware of the healing skills they are born with. Every one of you Number 6 people will start to be aware of your precious talent and by the time you enter into your third cycle—usually after the age of 36—you will be increasingly engaged in the work of uplifting the spirits of others, especially during hard times. Some of you do this through direct volunteer social work while others accomplish this in other ways. Your highest potential is in restoring balance to sick individuals and also to ailing communities.

Name Numbers 7, 8, and 9 *23*

Name Number 7: Magicians, philosophers

The number 7 is considered as a magic number in feng shui numerology, and those of you having names that reduce to a 7 will discover that the number also brings you unexpected or speculative luck, especially in your younger years. Number 7 people express themselves best by allowing their powerful mental skills to show themselves—these include exceptional memory power and the ability to concentrate so well that many seem to have psychic powers as well. Number 7s are therefore regarded as esoteric geniuses with extremely high IQs.

Not many people can hold a serious conversation with you, and especially not in any depth about religious or philosophical issues, so it is not surprising that you are a person of few words. Most of the time you do not bother communicating with others, but in your silence resides a powerful intellect that can be extremely powerful (and dangerous when used in a negative way.) You definitely can excel in metaphysical pursuits and can have a secret passion for the occult. You can also get obsessive about religion, especially during your older years.

Name Number 8: Wealth creators

Those whose Name Number 8 generally seem to possess more money luck than others. You are described as someone who has the ability to

generate material success energy, having the proverbial Midas touch! You express yourself best by creating prosperity, and this is because you have a natural instinct for making money that is unrivaled by the other numbers.

Number 8 Name Number people have the potential to become extremely successful in business and politics. If you find yourself becoming a banker or a stockbroker, a deal-maker or otherwise involved in finance, it is likely that you will rise very quickly to the top of the game. As long as you are engaged in expanding your income and expanding your asset worth, you will find a natural fulfilment. In your older years you will either become very ruthless or very benevolent, depending on what you do with the proceeds of your life's work. But Number 8 people very rarely stop working. Making money is in their blood, and they get their high from it.

Name Number 9: Humanitarians

Those of you with 9 as the number derived from their names are the humanitarians of the world; Number 9's destiny usually lies within the sphere of charitable causes, and they possess great skill in getting people and funds organized in these directions. Number 9s tend to think of the greater good and they are often so involved in their causes that these become an end in themselves.

Those who discover their niche in the world can lead very fulfilled lives, while those who are still searching might find life very distracting indeed. If you are a Number 9 person, go ally yourself with a cause as this will bring you great personal satisfaction. You will also end up contributing to a worthwhile project, which will reveal your talent for this kind of work.

Number 8s have money-making in their blood, while Number 9s can make money for others.

24 Name Numbers 11 and 22

Name Number 22: Crusaders

You are the sort of person who is happiest when you can feel that you are expounding a cause that can change the world. Number 22 people tend to be very intense in their urge to bring about a better world. In Chinese numerology the number 22 is a powerful number that can work very positively or very negatively.

Name Number 22s are capable of manifesting great changes on the earth and they usually cause this to happen because of their great influence on the minds of the leaders of the world. You will usually find a Number 22 pulling the strings in many of the world's great projects whether they are of a social, economic, or environmental significance. Number 22s have very powerful minds, and they also have an inherent ability to know how to use their mind to actualize and manifest events according to their desires.

Name Number 11: Spiritualists and masters of the esoteric

Number 11s are conduits of spiritual and esoteric information, and you are people who can feel a great need to transform the world with your vision; you really want to play a meaningful role this way—serving mankind, giving something back.

Name Number 11 people are spiritual powerhouses, while 22s are considered great crusaders.

Many of you will find that at some stage in your life you will get involved in things that are decidedly spiritual or even religious; it is likely that you will be happiest when involved with advancing certain specific branches of esoteric information that may hitherto have remained secret to the world. You express yourself best through your spirituality. You will be drawn toward becoming some kind of cultural leader and find that practices that have to do with astrology, fortune telling, or (as in my own case) as a feng shui writer and teacher will strike a powerful chord within you.

Number 11s have an innate spiritual strength and awareness of the cosmic forces at work in the world. You are often able to inspire a transformative effect in other people's lives. Your highest potential in life is to lead others to enlightenment.

In this sense, Name Number 22 people are considered to be magicians capable of bringing lofty ideals into the mainstream of everyday living. If you are a Number 22 person, do pursue your inclinations concerning the potential of the mind. You will be very successful in creating special pathways towards fulfilling your own destiny.

Auspicious numbers in feng shui

In the study of Chinese numerology every number has its own special meaning—both good and bad. Learn the significance of every number and how each can invoked or diminished to benefit your own well being. See also how the numbers can combine to create especially talismanic two- and even three-digit numbers.

25 The contemporary energy of number 8— current prosperity

From the time you become conscious of the luck dimension in your life, you will discover that certain numbers somehow resonate in your life very noticeably; usually, by the time you reach your early twenties and you are at college or holding down your first job, a certain number will seem to frequently catch your attention.

This may be your house address number or your Name Number, or the number of your day of birth. For different people different dates resonate more strongly than others, and the best way to "know" what your lucky number is—that is the number that is somehow associated with good events happening—is to tune your consciousness to notice when good opportunities are coming your way.

Meanwhile, whatever your lucky number is, the more it resonates with the number that defines

Number 8 is the luckiest number for our present times, because it describes the Period of 8 in feng shui, which lasts until 2024.

Amethysts activate the Earth energy of 8.

the present, the more in alignment you will be with the energy of the here and now!

In feng shui, we are currently living through what we call the Period of 8; this means we are now in the part of the cycle when the number 8 reigns supreme, so that for literally everyone the number 8 brings great good fortune luck. If your Birth or Name Numbers are also 8, or if when you work out your feng shui Kua Number later this is also an 8, then this number will resonate very powerfully with your personal energy. While this may not bring you direct luck, it definitely makes everything you do connect more effectively with the energy of the current period.

Activate the presence of 8

Remember that 8 is an Earth element number, so crystals such as amethyst (see above) in the vicinity enhance and activate its energy. Fire elements, such as lights, will also strengthen its presence.

Also the number 8 physically looks like the Infinity sign ∞, so 8 brings the good fortune of abundance and wealth luck continuously. Once it gets energized, its cycle of luck just keeps moving along. This is the great attraction of generating its presence within your space. So simply wear the 8 as pendant jewelry or as a ring, or display it as a decorative object in your house, and it will attract good energy (see the crystal 8 image, opposite).

So for the rest of the Period of 8, it is an excellent idea to welcome the physical presence of 8 into your home. And for good measure do try and let all your important numbers—phone numbers and car numbers, for instance, end with 8! This is the luckiest number of current times!

Number 8 brings good fortune to others

It is more a question of degree of good luck, and this varies from person to person. Since we are currently in the Period of 8, which will last until February 4 2024, the number 8 is not only lucky it is also strong. This means that 8 possesses inherent vigor to not only bring good fortune but also withstand obstacles for those who know how to activate its presence and its energy.

The infinity sign and number 8— the mystical knot

26

If you want to activate the "power of 8" in your home, or in your office, do go in search of the 8 or infinity sign symbol—and better still if this is made of earth containing gold; the symbolism generated by the Earth and Metal elements brings exceedingly good feng shui.

Always place this infinity symbol upright (never place it lying down) to signify energy moving upward in the northeast corner of your office, your living room, or even at the northeast corner of your work desk, so it can bring you the great abundance of this Period of 8. The infinity sign will activate the direct spirit of this period, bringing with it the luck of wonderful health and also excellent relationships.

Please note that in this period health issues are exceedingly important since the Period of 8 will be a time when many new strains of diseases and illness will be discovered. When you are ade-

quately protected you will be safe-guarded from falling seriously ill. This will safeguard you (and your family) from incurring exorbitant medical bills.

Multiply the power with the mystical knot

The 8 symbol is multiplied three times when it is worn or displayed as the powerful mystical knot, itself a very powerful symbol of good fortune. It is for this reason that this wonderfully beautiful and meaningful symbol has become so popular in recent years. Since the start of Period 8 in 2004, the knot has come into its own so that just having it near you will bring you good fortune. The knot is one of the 8 auspicious signs beloved of practitioners of Tibetan Buddhism (see Tip 27).

If you want to activate the mystical knot for wealth luck, get a wallet that has the mystical knot attached to it. It is even more auspicious if the knot is made of yellow gold metal to signify the Metal element. This ensures that your wallet will always be filled with cash, in a never-ending cycle.

Another way to activate the power of the knot is to wear it as a gold or diamond pendant around your throat chakra, at the base of your neck. This activates the power of your speech so that your words have persuasive power—an excellent feng shui energizer for people engaged in sales positions. When your throat chakra is empowered, your speech has power!

The number 8 is present in the mystical knot.

This number 8 appears as a crystal embedded with auspicious flecks of gold to bring excellent good fortune.

27 The eight auspicious signs and their numbers

The number 8 can be very effectively invoked by displaying the powerful set of auspicious signs so popular with Tibetan Buddhists. Each of the eight signs are also associated with the numbers 1 to 9 (excluding the number 5, which is signified by the tai chi symbol of yin and yang).

The double fish bring protection and good luck. The lotus symbolizes purity.

1. **The Banner of Victory** brings the good fortune of being victorious over one's enemies and foes. So it helps those who are engaged in a competitive situation with others. This symbol does extremely well for those whose Birth or Name Number is 1.

2. **The Double Fish** brings the good fortune of abundance and also good descendants luck. This symbol is also regarded as a protective symbol by many people, who see the double fish as ensuring that all one's descendents stay safe and secure. In Thailand, a strongly Buddhist country, the double fish symbol is often given to children to wear as a protective talisman. This symbol resonates strongly for those whose Birth Number is 2.

3. **The Vase** brings the luck of peace and harmonious relationships into all your interactions with others. This is a wonderful symbol of things going right in your life, so aggravations are drastically reduced. The vase is one of the most popular symbols of peace and harmony. The number most often associated with the vase is the number 3; it reduces any aggravations brought by this number.

4. **The Lotus** is the sign of purity and it symbolizes the power of the highest motivation, that of others above the self. This sign is closely allied to the number 4, and to some it also signifies the good fortune of a happy family life.

5. **The Conch** is the symbol associated with good news. The sound of the conch transcends the dimensions of space and time so that as a symbolic representation of good fortune, the conch resonates with the number 6—providing a channel to the dimensions of the celestials.

6. **The Parasol** is the sign of protection and it is often associated with the number 7, since it offers protection from war, violence, and harmful people. When this symbol is present in your environment, it signifies safety from those who would harm you. In Chinese feng shui the umbrella has always been a symbol of protection.

7. **The Mystic Knot** brings the good fortune of never-ending happiness. The knot symbolizes a continuity of all the good things coming to make you happy and contented, and this includes prosperity, good relationships, love, romance, and marriage. This symbol does extremely well for those whose Birth or Name Number is 8.

8. **The Wheel** symbolizes the good fortune of having wisdom that reveals the true nature of reality, bringing happiness and bliss. This symbol is often associated with the number 9 as it signifies the completion of all things.

The Eight Offering Goddesses 28

Making offerings to deities helps ensure eight types of good fortune and protection, from wisdom to overcoming obstacles. Offerings are made at home altars, when a little of each offering is placed by a deity.

In Chinese feng shui there are eight major offerings that, when made to deities and especially to the Buddhas, are believed to bring excellent good fortune. These eight offerings each signify one of the eight aspirations that make up a good life. The eight offerings are:

1. Food offerings, which signify prosperity
2. Money offerings, which signify generosity that leads to wealth
3. Water offerings, which signify clear minds
4. Flower offerings, which signify beauty
5. Light offerings, which signify knowledge and wisdom
6. Incense offerings, which signify the overcoming of obstacles
7. Music or sound offerings, which signify happiness
8. Dance offerings, which signify a cause for celebration.

These items are associated with each of the Eight Offering Goddesses who bring blessings from the Buddha. The symbolism here is once again of the auspicious number eight, indicating that there is also a divine connection between this number and the celestial deities that shower down good-fortune blessings.

So for those of you who have an altar at home it is a good idea to enhance its energy by making offerings to the deities on your altar; and for good measure, place eight lovely figurines to signify the Eight Offering Goddesses.

29   The Eight Immortals

The most famous manifestation of the Taoist's high regard for the number 8 is associated with the legendary Eight Immortals. These are reputed to be special celestial beings who have gained Immortality. Each of these Immortals, or Taoist saints, are associated with the gift of good-luck empowerments and having their images in the home invokes the good-fortune energies associated with the Period of 8, one of nine time periods linked to the time dimension of feng shui.

As the world is currently said to be living through the Period of 8, the number 8 has become incredibly auspicious for everyone; so therefore it

Placing a figurine of the Eight Immortals in your home invites the powerful energies of the Period of 8.

The eight talismans of the Eight Immortals

When images of the Eight Immortals crossing the great waters are placed inside homes, they help residents go through struggles and bad luck to eventually emerge victorious; having them in the home during the Period of 8 is also an excellent way of activating the power of 8. Their presence in the home is also believed to activate the talismans that they each hold, and these are said to be the source of their great powers. Thus:

- Zhang Guolao's **drum** will help to bring a good name to the family
- Lu Dongbin's **sword** will help to subdue all physical afflictions
- Han Xingzi's **flute** will bring important growth and development luck
- He Xiangu's **water lily** will encourage the luck of the family to bloom
- Tie Guaili's **gourd** will bring healing energy to those who are sick
- Zhong Liquan's **fan** will offer protection from people with bad intentions
- Ao Guojiu's **jade disc** will improve the feng shui of the environment
- Lan Caihe's **flower basket** will bring beauty and happiness

is extremely auspicious to invite images of the Eight Immortals into the home.

There are many legends associated with the Eight Immortals, but perhaps the most famous of all is the legend of the Immortals crossing the sea, a voyage when their skills and their "powers" are sorely tested, a journey that has come to manifest the changes that we all live through and experience, as we maneuver our way through life.

The Eight Immortals also separately represent the two genders—male and female—the old, the young, the rich, the poor, and the noble and the humble. So according to legend, everyone from all levels of society, can benefit from the eight celestial beings. Once again then, having them in the home will highlight the power of the auspicious number 8.

The magnifying power of number 9— future prosperity

30

In Chinese feng shui, another extremely auspicious number—that in the current Period of 8 signifies future posterity—is the number 9. This number is auspicious on its own and it is often associated with the color purple. Those with the Birth Number 9 have a very special relationship with this number; it is a number of completion, a number that magnifies.

The number 9 is associated with many auspicious legends and is a number that is steadfast and never deviates. Multiplied any number of times, 9 always adds up to 9—no matter how many times it is repeated, the sum of 9 always adds up to 9. This makes the number incorruptible. Thus 9 x 9 is 81 which adds up to 9, and 9 times 3 is 27 which also adds up to 9. This mathematical phenomenon of 9 demonstrates its completion quality—9 is a number that is unchanging and steadfast. It is also very powerful.

Dragons and phoenixes

To the Chinese the number 9 is most often associated with the nine dragons and the nine phoenixes and in Beijing many public places have the all powerful nine dragon screen made in porcelain. The placement of the nine dragons—for instance in the Imperial palace of the Forbidden City, in Hebei Park and in other prominent places of the city in the recent twenty years—is one of the most telling pieces of evidence that indicate that feng shui has come back to China and is now attracting an increasing number of practitioners. For many years, under Mao Tse Tung, feng shui had been practiced only clandestinely but with the new freedoms sweeping across China feng shui has once again become trendy. Hence the nine dragons have re-emerged!

Meanwhile the direction associated with 9 is south and the creature most often identified with 9 is the horse. Thus to activate the number 9 in your life, it is an excellent idea to invite in any of these auspicious creatures—

Nine is a number that magnifies other numbers and indicates completion.

dragon, phoenix or horse—but in 9s or multiples of 9. Paintings and screens featuring these creatures bring excellent feng shui for those whose Birth or Name Number is 9. Note that 9 is thus in many ways even luckier than 8 and definitely longer-lasting.

There are also nine levels leading to the state of perfect happiness, and when nine is paired with any number it has the power to magnify the power of the other number.

The phoenix and dragon are auspicious number 9 creatures when displayed in multiples of that number.

31 The number 6—unexpected "heaven" luck

The number 6 is often associated with the state of heaven and the personality of the benevolent leader. In terms of elements the number 6 is associated with Big Metal; it is also a white number that is regarded very favorably indeed.

The number 6 possesses a divine power that can overcome earthly afflictions, so when wind chimes are made with six rods they become more powerful for overcoming and subduing all the intangible afflictions brought by the changing energies of each new year. Wind chimes that have six rods also possess the power to subdue the bad luck of illness and misfortunes and are often used to ward off the illness-bearing stars of annual feng shui charts.

Number 6 is associated with the luck of heaven.

Also, waterfall features designed for the living room to enhance wealth luck are more effective when the waterfall has six or nine tiers for the water to fall! Thus note that a six-tier or a nine-tier waterfall is always to be preferred over other water features.

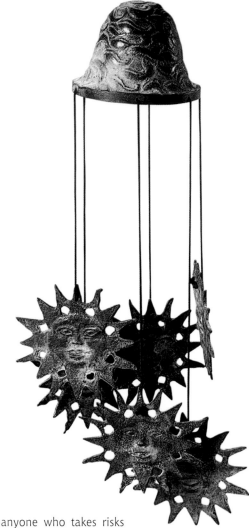

Bring the luck of 6 into your life

It is an excellent idea for those whose Birth or Name Number resonates with 6 to invite this number into their life. For instance, use the 6 in the numbers that mean something to you. Get car numbers and phone numbers to resonate with 6 if this is the number that brings you good fortune. Remember that 6 is the number that attracts unexpected luck. It is particularly suitable for

anyone who takes risks or gambles. The number 6 brings unexpected feng shui luck! Sometimes this luck can be described as being something of a windfall!

There are those who believe that when you use the number 6 it invokes the help of the celestials and for those who appreciate speculative luck it is a good idea to activate this number by hanging wind chimes with 6 rods or have a water feature with water falling over 6 levels.

The number 4—good or bad luck?   32

To residents of Hong Kong and Canton who are conscious of the importance of feng shui, the number 4, which sounds like the word "die" in Cantonese, is most times frowned upon. Hence this is a number that enjoys little acceptance or favor either in car numbers, or in addresses and telephone numbers. Indeed to the Hong Kong Chinese the number 4 should be avoided at all costs; thus level 4 in apartment blocks and office buildings is usually very hard to rent out.

In recent years, however, as knowledge of real feng shui has spread and people have become more knowledgeable, the number 4 has lost much of its bad press. Now it is more widely known that the number 4 brings romance luck, the kind of romance that can lead to marriage and family. The number 4 is also a number associated with the advancement of knowledge; hence it is a scholastic number of sorts.

Activate good fortune with the number 4

As such, if your Name Number or Birth Number is 4, it can and should be activated in your life to bring you good fortune. Thus, for instance, feng shui experts now encourage their clients to plant the four-season flowers and trees to ensure that good fortune is enjoyed throughout the four seasons of a year. This translates to symbolize continuous good fortune irrespective of the weather or the season.

In fact the old-style traders and tycoons of Hong Kong often insist that there should be paintings that denote the splendor of each of the four seasons hanging in their offices to ensure that good luck in business continues through the four seasons of the year, not just during Spring or Summer alone. This was believed to ensure profits stay on course through the year.

Number 4 relates to luck in romantic endeavors.

The power of numbers 1 and 11   33

There is always something very special about the number 1 and when it is doubled or tripled into 11 or 111, anyone associated with it in any way will enjoy the luck of winning, of having the potential to emerge as a winner in any competitive situation they might enter.

This usually refers to those whose Birth or Name Numbers are 1 or 11; those born on January 1, January 11, November 1, and, better yet, on November 11 will also discover that the numbers 1 and 11 are likely to bring them wealth and success luck.

It is especially good to live in a house whose address features the numbers 1 or 11—such as in Road 1 or with a house number that is 1 or 11. When in school, the numbers 1 and 11 will also bring excellent luck in your studies. To activate these numbers, it is an excellent idea to create the presence of 11 in your home space, more particularly on your desk for those wanting good career luck. The number 1 is also the alpha of numbers, thereby symbolizing the first number of the universal cosmic force.

Eleven resonates with being a winner—the power of two number 1s.

34 The special "wholeness" of 18 and 9 multiples

The numbers 18, 81, 27, 72, 36, 63, 45, and 54 are numbers that add up to nine and these are also the result of multiplying the number 9 any number of times—they always add up to nine.

Thus to invoke the power of the number 9 it is a good idea to look for combinations that add up to nine as a single digit number. The power of the universe is also believed to be encapsulated in numbers that add up to the ultimate nine, so that feng shui formulas that use the powers of numerology to interpret the quality of sectors within the home assign a special "wholeness" to this kind of number combination;

It is regarded as the completion number and at the present time frame in the feng shui reckoning of time, the number 9 stands for "future prosperity"; that is bringing wealth luck for the future. And being the omega of numbers, it has an affinity with the number 1, which is the alpha of numbers; such a combination not only creates the auspiciousness of the sum of ten, but it also signifies beginning and the completion luck, and so is necessary in any endeavour.

Nine and completion luck

The Chinese refer to 9 as signifying the existence of completion luck, so that whoever invokes the power of 9 is ensuring that whatever gets started also gets completed in a lucky way. You can activate the power of 9 inside your home by hanging nine of any auspicious symbol such as a nine-dragon screen; or a painting that shows nine horses; of keeping nine goldfish in an aquarium.

It is also auspicious to place a nine-level waterfall in the southeast corner to activate wealth accumulation luck; or a nine-rod metal wind chime in the northwest to create good fortune for the house patriarch. Activating the nine also ensures that good fortune is long-lasting, as nine also signifies stable future prosperity.

Nine fish will bring the luck of future prosperity to a home.

The power of number 22 and other doubles   35

The power of doubles is something Taoists repeatedly stress as being exceptionally lucky, especially to ensure good harmony and happiness within the family. When there is a pair of anything symbolic it always activates the good fortune of having a happy relationship between mother and father, husband and wife!

These are the premier figures in the family unit and they are also regarded as the source of a family's health and happiness, with the father symbolizing the source of the family's wealth and good fortune and the mother symbolizing the nurturing care. When there is a pair of everything used to decorate the home, it ensures the presence, well-being, and safety of both a mother and father figure.

Display pairs of celestial protectors

Thus celestial protectors—dragons, horses, fu dogs, and so forth—must be present inside the home as a pair, male and female, if they are to bring the energy of togetherness; meanwhile other meaningful symbols such as vases, birds, and crystal balls are also best when displayed as a pair.

The number 22 can represent the security of a mother and father figure in the home. Other pairs, like the two fu dogs (below left) reinforce this presence.

At the same time the doubling of lucky numbers also has positive feng shui significance. For instance, according to Taoist principles on good luck, when your Birth Number is doubled—in other words occurs twice as in 11, 22, 33, 44, and so on—this doubles the luck it brings you.

This concept of "double goodness" is reflected in many Taoist feng shui recommendations and in the current Period of 8 you should not be surprised to see the number 88 being used repeatedly by those wanting to energize the power of 8. This is because the number 8 is regarded as the universally lucky number from now on until the year 2024!

36 What 28 means and other sum-of-ten combinations

One of the most highly revered "specials" in the use of numbers in feng shui is all the lucky connotations associated with the number combinations that create the "sum-of-ten." Thus combinations of 1 and 9, 2 and 8, 3 and 7, 4 and 6, and the double 5—each of which adds up to 10—are favored combinations, believed to bring all-round luck for anyone, attracting whatever luck may be missing, or badly needed, at any moment in time. The sum-of-ten features prominently in feng shui numerology and there are some powerful formulas associated with it in time-dimension feng shui.

Do you benefit from the sum-of-ten?

When the sum-of-ten is present in your date of birth, especially when embedded in your Birth Number, it indicates a hidden potential of success luck that is also complete. The sum of ten signifies having everything, especially abundance, because the number 10 gets reduced to 1, the premier number.

For instance, those born on September 1, or January 9, would have the 1 and 9 embedded in their Birth Number. Here we use the day and the month of birth to create the sum-of-ten within the Birth Number. Likewise, if you were born on February 8, the second month of the year, you will benefit from the sum-of-ten combination.

Is the sum-of-ten part of your Birth Number?

If you do have this special combination as part of your Birth Number, it is a good idea to check whether it becomes your lucky number. For this you will need to observe whether good things happen to you on days associated with the combination you have.

For instance, if your sum-of-ten number is 28 (born on February 8 or on the August 2, or if you were born on the 28th of any month, making the number 28 significant for you) then you should start to observe whether lucky things happen to you that are associated with number 28—such as when you were promoted, did you know about it on a day associated with 28? Were you 28 years old when you married, or is your house number 28? Or if you bet on that number, does it uncannily work for you every time? Or do investments and contracts signed on the 28th work out well for you? Did you meet someone important that day?

Once you start living in a state of conscious awareness of the numbers that "fly" into your life, you will begin to see patterns of luck associated with specific number combinations—good as well as bad luck. And of course once you become aware of your lucky number, stick with it; the good stuff a lucky number or combination of numbers brings really does get better over the years.

"Big auspicious" brought by 168 combination   37

In time-dimension feng shui there are few numbers luckier than the combination of the powerful white numbers 1, 6, and 8. These three numbers each have lucky connotations: 1 is the winner's number, 6 the heavenly number, and 8 the current number of prosperity. But when they occur in your date of birth, made up of the day, month, and year single digits, they are said to be deeply embedded in your Birth Number.

Anyone who has 1, 6, and 8 embedded in their birth date will enjoy outstanding luck in their careers or business. There is wealth to be made and incomes expand and grow with the years, especially when the number gets energized by having its preference in your physical world. This can occur as car numbers, telephone numbers, house address numbers, and so forth. The three numbers can occur in an any order. They are equally lucky whether as 861 or 681 or 618 or 168… The three numbers signify Earth producing Metal producing Water—so ultimately they bring wealth and abundance.

The luck brought is "big auspicious," which means that the opportunities that this number brings to you can lead to important success that has long-term positive implications.

If you do have this combination in your birth date it pays to systematically create its presence around you as much as possible. You can even wear this as a lucky number charm pendant!

Majong counters read "1, 6, 8" in Cantonese.

Using all the lucky numbers   38

Those who have different Birth and Name Numbers should observe which of the two numbers brings them better luck. Over time this will become obvious to you—and if neither of the two numbers bring any noticeable good fortune, then you will need to investigate the embedded numbers within the birth date. You might also need to rethink your Name Number as you could have got this wrong.

For some people, however, their lucky number is their Kua Number—which is worked out using their gender and their lunar date of birth (see Tip 85). I have discovered that for many people, in terms of bringing luck, it is this Kua Number that seems more powerful. But when this is the same as the Birth or Name Number, then the concept of double goodness gets activated!

Similarly it is also the special numbers that are embedded within the birth date that provide hidden good luck. The key is to correctly identify the number or number combinations that work best for you. This usually cannot be verified until one is well into middle age, since you need enough years of observation to confirm to yourself what your lucky numbers are. If you have not yet identified your lucky number or numbers, use your Birth and Name Numbers to point you in the right direction.

Using both your Birth and Name Numbers intensifies your luck.

Favorable and unfavorable dimensions

Before you begin to use your own personal numbers you can start to use the auspicious dimensions found on the feng shui ruler to improve the chi energy in your home. If you remember that there are also unfavorable dimensions, to avoid incorporating the lucky dimensions is the first step towards putting the feng shui study of numbers into effect.

The feng shui ruler 39

The practice of feng shui recognizes that there are favorable and unfavorable dimensions, and in the days of the emperors court carpenters charged with making imperial furniture were meticulous in ensuring that every throne, chair, table, or cabinet made for palace use would conform to the imperial feng shui ruler of prosperous dimensions. For a long time these auspicious and inauspicious dimensions—which were laid out in a feng shui ruler—were known only within court circles, but with the decline of dynastic rule in China many imperial secrets have now become available to everyone.

Using the ruler

Today the feng shui ruler with its auspicious dimensions is freely available and anyone can now avail themselves of its secrets. It can be used to measure tables, cupboards, windows, and doors to ensure that their dimensions are auspicious.

When you sit on a chair and work from a desk with auspicious dimensions, good luck gets activated for you automatically and this happens every day that you use the chair and table! Auspicious dimensions can be applied in almost every aspect of your daily life and living, so calling cards, as well as windows, doors, and furniture can be designed according to favorable dimensions.

Once you understand the cycle of dimensions you will discover that there are hundreds of ways to use these lucky dimensions. For instance in addition to furniture, doors and windows, you can also use lucky dimensions on photo frames, feng shui decorative objects, books, posters, and so forth. You can basically use lucky dimensions to enhance almost everything and indeed lucky and unlucky dimensions can be applied to patterns and design proportions.

But first you should understand what the dimensions themselves mean.

You can purchase a metal feng shui ruler or a feng shui tape measure (below), from most online feng shui stores.

How the feng shui ruler works

The way the ruler is designed, it has eight cycles of dimensions, four of which are auspicious and four inauspicious. The challenge to the practitioner is to design space and objects in a way that adheres only to the lucky dimensions, though these favorable dimensions can get as small or as large as you wish because the system is all to do with proportions!

Each cycle measures the equivalent of 17in or 43cm, and each cycle is categorized into eight segments. The cycle of lucky and unlucky dimensions then repeats itself over and over again to infinity.

The red segments shown on this feng shui tape measure represent the four auspicious dimensions—Chai, Yi, Kwan, and Pun—whereas the black

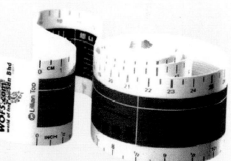

segments correspond to the four inauspicious dimensions—Pi, Li, Chieh, and Hai.

CHAI	PI	YI	LI	KWAN	CHIEH	PUN	HAI

40 Lucky dimensions of the feng shui ruler

When you look closely at the meanings of the auspicious dimensions you will note that all four of the range of auspicious measurements bring success and wealth luck!

The feng shui ruler has four lucky dimensions that bring prosperity.

Chai dimensions

Chai dimensions lie between 0–2⅛in (0–5.4cm). This is the first segment of the lucky cycle and it brings wealth luck. It is subdivided into four categories of good luck. The first approximate half-inch brings money luck; the second brings a safe filled with jewels; the third brings together six types of good fortune, while the fourth brings abundance. So this first lucky segment of Chai brings variations of prosperity luck and if you want to activate directly for good wealth luck use multiples of this dimension!

Pun dimensions promise plenty of jewelry and great prosperity luck.

Yi dimensions

Yi dimensions are from 6⅜–8½in (16.2–21.5cm). This is the fourth segment of the cycle. It brings overall mentor luck—it attracts helpful people into your life and ensures a continuity of your family name and fortune. Again there are four sub-sectors. The first approximate half-inch means excellent descendants luck; the second predicts unexpected added income from influential sources; the third predicts a very successful successor son and the fourth offers excellent mentor influence luck.

Kwan dimensions

Kwan dimensions are 8½–10⅝in (21.5–27cm). This fifth segment of the cycle brings power and wealth luck. The first sub-sector means you will pass all tests and exams easily; the second sub-sector predicts special or speculative luck; the third offers vastly and sudden improved income; the fourth attracts high honors for the family.

Pun dimensions

Pun dimensions are 14⅝–17in (37.5–43.2cm), the eighth segment of the cycle. This category of dimension brings overall a great flow of wealth coming in, and particularly so for the first sub-sector of Pun. The second sub-sector spells luck in important examinations; the third predicts plenty of jewelry, and the fourth offers abundant prosperity. Hence this range of dimensions also bring wealth luck. And since this leads seamlessly back to a repeat of the first set of lucky dimensions, which also spell luck, there is great deal of leeway for playing with these dimensions so an entire house can be built incorporating wealth dimensions.

CHAI   YI   KWAN   PUN

Unlucky dimensions of the feng shui ruler   41

The four unlucky dimensions of the ruler bring a host of misfortune luck ranging from illness to loss of wealth. It is thus advisable to try and avoid having these unlucky dimensions on any of the furniture that you use.

Pi dimensions

Pi dimensions are 2⅛–4⅖in (5.4–10.8cm). This category brings loss of money and illness. The first approximate half-inch implies income being lowered and reducing, so money retreats; the second indicates legal problems associated with money; the third brings losing a legal battle and even going to jail! The fourth indicates death of a spouse. This set of dimensions is extremely severe

in its bad luck and should thus be strenuously avoided!

Li dimensions

Li dimensions are between 4⅖–6⅜in (10.8–16.2cm). This category means separation from your wealth; the first half-inch means a store of bad luck resulting in loss of wealth, while the second predicts direct loss of money. The third says you will meet up with unscrupulous people who cheat you, and the fourth predicts being a victim of theft or burglary.

Chieh dimensions

Chieh dimensions are between 10⅝–12⅝in (27–32.4cm). This category of bad dimension spells total loss. The first approximate half-inch spells the death of someone important or a departure of some kind; the second that everything you need will disappear, and you could lose your livelihood; the third indicates you will be chased out of your village in disgrace, and the fourth indicates a very severe loss of money. This is an even more severe case of bad luck—the main door should never have these dimensions!

Hai dimensions

Hai dimensions are between 12⅝–14⅝in (32.4–37.5cm). These dimensions indicate severe bad luck starting with obstacles blocking success in the first sub-sector, loss of loved one in the second, sicknesses and ill health in the third, and scandal and quarrels in the fourth sector.

Check your work desk for unlucky dimensions as this could affect your influence and success in a negative way.

The measurements of the main door of your home should never fall within Chieh dimensions, which spells total loss and misfortune.

| PI | | LI | | CHIEH | | HAI | |

42 Using the feng shui ruler

Once you have familiarized yourself with the use of the feng shui cycle of dimensions you can apply it to almost everything to improve your prosperity luck. Dimensions address the material side of luck so good dimensions usually bring prosperity or the circumstances that lead to prosperity.

For this reasons it is also vital to ensure that your dimensions do *not* bring misfortune luck. In fact those who are experienced in feng shui, always apply this cardinal principle to their use of this ancient practice. They understand that feng shui always guards against the occurrence of misfortunes and helps prevent reversal of fortunes. Thus the feng shui ruler is as much for showing us good dimensions as it is for indicating the dimensions that could, over the medium to long-term, bring misfortune luck.

If necessary, opt for a comfortable table height rather than a good feng shui height, and incorporate feng shui dimensions in other items instead.

The dimensions of prosperity

However, knowing the exact measurements and proportions of good fortune is one thing and actually using these dimensions can sometimes prove difficult. For instance windows and doors and furniture often have "standard" heights, widths, and depth. If these standards are of inauspicious dimensions it might sometimes prove difficult to overcome unless you are prepared to arrange for custom-built doors and windows. It is the same with furniture—desks at work, as well as dining tables—be they round or rectangular.

From a feng shui perspective we always want to be able to get the perfect rectangle, circle, or square—and often this implies they have to be custom-made and thus can be much more expensive than the standard dimension tables. Another problem is the height of tables. You will find that auspicious feng shui heights for tables tend to be too high at 33in (82.5cm) as the standard comfortable table height is 30in (75cm). Thus not everyone will find feng shui dimensions are good for them. The advice here is to use as much with auspicious dimensions as you are able to; but go for comfort. When the feng shui heights are unsuitable for you, it makes more sense to opt for what is comfortable.

43 Using the ruler to enhance business cards

The dimensions given in the ruler can also be used to help you make auspicious business cards. The problem with business cards, however, is that it is not possible to find an auspicious dimension for both sides of the card—to have a card with lucky measurements means it will end up either too long or too wide. In this case it is enough that just one side of the card adopts the lucky dimension. Do make certain, however, that there are no lines on your business card because these tend to set up invisible parameters that block your luck.

Using the ruler to surround your image with lucky chi 44

Perhaps the best use of the lucky dimension ruler is to use it to make auspicious picture frames. Surrounding your image or that of your family with prosperity-bringing dimensions creates excellent feng shui for all the members of your family. Choose dimensions that resonate with your aspirations whether this be wealth, good relationships, or for achieving high honors in exams.

Thus photo frames can have a width between 6⅜–8½ in (16.2–21.5 cm) as this range of dimensions brings excellent mentor luck, good children, and influential friends luck. The indications for these dimensions benefit the family extensively so these are excellent for family photographs.

As for the length of the picture frame this can be between 8½–10⅝ inches (21.5–27cm). With this dimension, students benefit greatly since it helps them pass examinations with flying colors. For the rest of the family this range of measurements brings high honors and vastly improved income luck.

This is such an important point that I have designed a collection of picture frames using auspicious dimensions to aid in the creation of excellent feng shui for you and your family. Remember that when you have a picture showing all members of the family smiling broadly and happily there is no better way of creating harmony and safety for the family.

Pay attention to the frame dimensions of photographs.

Using a picture frame is one of the easiest contemporary ways to create good feng shui for the whole family. When you add the extra factor of dimension luck, it becomes even more effective.

Using the ruler to create auspicious cupboards 45

In the old days special cabinets were made that followed feng shui dimensions and were decorated with auspicious symbols such as lucky flowers and plants, as well as celestial protectors, and this was believed to bring good fortune energy chi to the robes and tunics worn by members of the aristocracy, and of course the Emperor's family.

The Chinese always guarded their apparel with great care as they believed they would be affected negatively should the clothes they wore be afflicted by bad energy. Since cabinets contained everything worn on the body they had to have good feng shui. So lucky dimensions became an essential part of furniture making!

Today you can do the same, and have all your custom-built cupboards and cabinets created according to the lucky dimensions of the feng shui ruler.

If custom-made closets are an option, have them built with feng shui dimensions in mind.

46 Room proportions according to the Magic Ratio

This little-known formula in feng shui brings amazing results and it is referred to in the ancient texts as the Magic Ratio of dimensions. Easy to understand and simple to apply, it is used for arranging furniture in homes and offices.

The origins of this ratio go back thousands of years and it reflects the essence of the lucky numbers 1, 6, and 8, which I love so much and have so much faith in. This divine ratio has also been described in the old texts as celestial proportions of space that have the power to create feelings of calm and happiness, bringing excellent feng shui to all who live and work within. Once you understand the basis of how it is used you can very easily apply this formula to bring greater good fortune, peace, and even spiritual awakenings into your living and work space. Any home, big or small, apartment or house, studio or condominium can benefit from this formula.

This is a very easy way to make your feng shui "right" and all that is required is for you to organize your space in such a way that its proportions correspond according to the celestial proportions of heavenly feng shui. When you create your space according to these proportions—when you arrange your furniture, hang pictures on your walls, create color schemes, or place plants

Using the Magic Ratio at home is amazingly simple, and spaces that conform to this ratio will be naturally lucky.

in a way that make your room, garden, or office visibly reflect these proportions—you will instantly feel a difference in yourself. Your attitudes will become more positive, your family becomes more harmonious, and good things start to happen for you. Luck starts to flow magically into your life!

What exactly is the Magic Ratio?

The basis of the idea is to create spaces that conform to the ratio of 1:1.618. To remember this formula think of the numbers 1, 6, 8—these are the three "white" numbers in feng shui that collectively resonate with the cosmic universe, unlocking the channels that enable divine energy to flow into your space. The ancients all knew about the power of this ratio and the Chinese feng shui masters of old incorporated this into their bag of space-arrangement formulas.

Applying the ratio means that irrespective of the dimensions and shape of any room—such as rooms you spend a great deal of time in, which can be your home or your office—if you make a special effort to create a visibly discernible space that conforms to this ratio, the space instantly becomes luckier.

The Magic Ratio

To harness the power of the Magic Ratio, create spaces that conform to the ratio of 1:1.618: just think of the numbers 1, 6, 8. The diagram shows the Ratio in action.

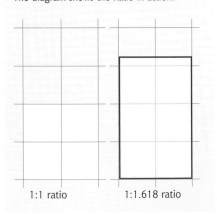

1:1 ratio   1:1.618 ratio

Applying the Magic Ratio to living areas   47

Measure the breadth of the room. Then multiply the shorter measurement by 1.618 to find the exact length the room should be. Then, create areas within the total space that conform to the width and the required length according to the ratio. It's as simple as that!

For instance, if the width of the living room is 10ft, then the length should ideally be 16.18 ft—creating the magic space! If a room is overly long, you need to define the space created by the ratio's proportions. So as a result the original long room becomes subtly divided into two visible areas.

If your room is 16ft wide, then the ideal space will be created by having a length of 16 x 1.618 = 25.8ft. It is not necessary to be perfectly exact in your measurements. Stay within the proportions indicated by the Magic Ratio as much as you can, but a small difference of an inch or so is acceptable. Then when you are doing your work, entertaining or just living in that space, you will feel the beneficial effects of good feng shui.

In the home
You can use this ratio to create good proportions for exceptionally long rooms, or to feng shui a narrow area that you wish to brighten up. As soon as you create the celestial proportions indicated, feelings of being constricted or squeezed in will disappear. Obstacles in your life also start to vanish. Success comes more easily in all that you do.

You can use any existing pillar to establish your dimensions, or use a defining color on walls to reflect the required proportions or to create a particular desired length. You can use furniture to emphasize the division; a side board or heavier piece of furniture makes a perfect natural divider that effectively marks out the visual length of any room. As soon as the space is created, you will find that it instantly feels good. In the home, the living room and the bedroom should be created according to this Magic Ratio.

In the office
In the office, use carpets and walls to mark out the space correctly and, if you are renovating your office, creating rooms according to the Magic Ratio will attract success luck. The ratio also applies to the office foyer, as this is where chi enters to flow within. Establish the visual effect of the proportion and see your feng shui improve! Employees feel happier, cooperate more effectively, and become a lot more productive.

In the garden
No matter how small your garden, you can create celestial proportions using plants, hedges and small bushes. In Malaysia and Singapore, where plants grow so fast, it is easy to use the garden to create good feng shui for the home. Well-maintained gardens create the "bright hall" that attracts good chi, so it is worth making the effort. All you need do is measure the correct length and width of a designated space, then work from there. Those living in apartments can use their balconies to create celestial space according to the ratio, then place growing plants there to activate the space!

Magic Ratio spaces feel naturally right as soon as you walk into them. Check your outside spaces for Magic Ratio proportions too, from decking areas to balconies.

48 How the Magic Ratio transcends cultures

The proportions of the Parthenon reflect the Magic Ratio.

Now let me tell you about a wonderful coincidence—although, of course, nothing in life is a coincidence. Pythagoras, the ancient Greek mathematician, was a genius in his time. His works on numbers reflect many celestial and divine laws of numerology from many cultures. He discovered a ratio he called "the Golden Mean," which corresponds exactly with the Magic Ratio of China's feng shui texts! This was for me a very exciting discovery.

He describes the rectangle that is created by using the measurements of the Magic Ratio as the Golden Rectangle. This shape, he says, is most beneficial for the welfare of human beings. Since then, wise men have discovered this ratio resonating everywhere in nature, from the spirals of the conch shell to the proportion of petals in specific flowers.

Ancient architects have also incorporated these proportions into some of the most famous buildings that have stood the test of time. Thus it has been discovered that the pyramids at Cheops contain chambers within that correspond to the Golden Mean, especially the King's chamber whose measurements correspond exactly to the ratio; and in Greece the Parthenon, the great temple on the Acropolis also has dimensions that reflect this magical ratio of 1:1.618. The same divine measurements can be found in the Taj Mahal in India, as well as within ancient cathedrals in France and Poland.

49 Other ways to use the 1:1.168 ratio

You can be as creative as you wish in using the Magic Ratio, as it applies to every dimension of living. Thus you can ensure that the frames that contain family portraits hanging on the walls of your home also reflect this divine ratio. This brings excellent good feng shui to those whose pictures are contained within the frame. You can use a lucky dimension for one side of the frame and then use it to create the ratio to make a perfect rectangle. You can also create a Golden Rectangular mirror using the ratio and use this mirror to reflect yourself when you get dressed for work. Framing yourself within the ratio each morning is a powerful feng shui ritual. I have used this throughout my life, and it ensures that you will always look attractive in the eyes of others.

- Look for rectangular dining tables that reflect these proportions or, better yet, make one that can seat six or eight people. This is a perfect example of excellent feng shui furniture.
  - Place a coffee table in the living room that has this ratio
  - Create a balcony of plants according to the ratio.

The ideas for using the Magic Ratio are endless, so you can be as creative as you wish.

Find a mirror that conforms to the Magic Ratio, and use it every morning for personal empowerment.

Numbers in house feng shui

Every house has its own chart depending on when it was built and which way it faces. By learning how to read the chart numbers and discover their significance you will be able to activate the favorable ones while subduing the effects of those that spell danger. The annual changes will affect the charts, so you will also discover how to update your home so that it is always at full strength.

50 Feng shui house charts

There is a powerful feng shui formula that expresses the secrets of house luck in numbers. Thus, numbers from 1 to 9 are placed in a three-by-three square grid that is then overlaid on a building floorplan to mark out the luck of different sectors of any house, creating a chart of numbers known as a feng shui house chart. This method of feng shui has always been extremely popular in Hong Kong and Taiwan, In recent years it has enjoyed a major revival in China as the country opens up to embrace the traditional cultural influences of its past once again. In the world outside China, many practitioners of feng shui are also beginning to discover the magic of the numbers of the feng shui house chart.

This method of feng shui is sometimes referred to as flying star feng shui with the numbers being likened to "stars" that bring good or bad luck. By using flying stars to assess the luck of different parts of the home, we address changes of chi energy over time. We read the luck by studying the feng shui house charts.

Each specially constructed house charts reveals the secrets of energy within any building, with the luck of each sector expressed by numbers. There are numbers to denote wealth luck, relationship luck, health luck, and so forth while others also offer timely warnings of illness, afflictive situations, accidents, and misfortunes. There is therefore an element of forecasting that predicts possible misfortunes in this method of feng shui, so it is an extremely useful numerology aspect of feng shui practice that is extremely beneficial to learn and use to improve one's overall luck.

Let the sectors govern your home

Different numbers in each sector of the house chart will forecast different types of luck, so there are combinations of two or three numbers that reveal the quality of house luck.

This method of feng shui also tracks the changes of energy over time as the Chinese have always believed in this concept. Everyone's luck changes with the passage of time and the challenge of feng shui is to keep track of the changes of energy so that we are then able to protect ourselves against times of bad luck, as well as enhance the energies surrounding us during periods of good fortune.

Each feng shui house chart, or "flying star" chart, is linked with the time a house was built or renovated and its facing direction. It reveals a home's luck expressed using the numbers 1 to 9.

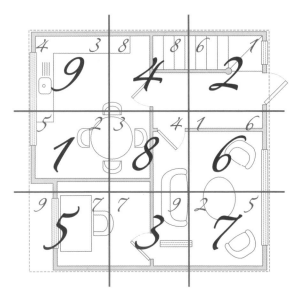

We are currently in the Period of 8 51

The flying Star method of feng shui recognizes cycles of time periods that last 20 years. Each of these periods is ruled by a number and characterized by the attributes associated with that number. We are currently in the Period of 8, a very lucky number associated with the image of the mountain, the trigram Ken, and the youngest son of the family.

The Period of 8 started on February 4 2004 and with the change in period came many changes in the energies of the world. Many countries experienced changes in leadership. Tastes, fads, and fashions also changed as did business models and ways of getting rich. In these past few years since the start of Period 8, the world has seen many and sudden changes and also experienced transformational paradigm shifts in the economic and psychological environments of the world. In fact the global village as a concept has become a reality as travel and communications have cut through centuries old barriers, fueled as much by technological breakthroughs as by new discoveries and inventions. The Internet and the computer have digitalized communications to such an extent that the world has shrunk and we must now look to the stars and outer space to see the bigger picture of our universe!

The auspicious period

All this has happened in this particular Period of 8, an age of the mountain which reveals so much new knowledge to us. The world and all of us within it must adjust to a new kind of energy, the Period 8 energy. The number 8 has always been viewed as an auspicious number that promises wealth and success; but now it is also the number that signifies new knowledge and an ever-widening circle of connectivity that is sure to have repercussions. It is thus very beneficial to resonate along with it. Tap into it, using it to enhance your life because the number 8 is the key to unlocking the luck of this new period!

There are altogether nine periods of 20 years each, so the full cycle of feng shui time lasts 180 years. In each 20-year period, there is a reigning number and the ruling number of the current period is 8. In its own period, the ruling number reigns supreme and is extremely auspicious. So in the current period of 8, the number 8 takes on that mantle of auspiciousness—being very strong and very vigorous. Utilize this number as much as you can to benefit from the energies of the current period!

Period 8 is known as the "age of the mountain." The number 8 will be lucky until the year 2024.

52 Changing your house into a Period 8 house

One of the most important things you need to know about feng shui is that the passage of time has an immensely powerful effect on luck.

The time factor influences the energy of houses to a very significant extent so this is something that feng shui practitioners in Hong Kong and Singapore always factor into their practice. Many have already changed their homes into what we term Period of 8 homes because they know how important this is to maintaining their good fortune.

Transforming the house you live in to a Period of 8 house is absolutely necessary to rejuvenate the energies of your home (and office). If you really want to benefit from good feng shui it is vital that you transform your home into a Period of 8 home as soon as possible. This is the key, the secret to preserving your good fortune. Unless you change the energy of your home and make it into a Period of 8 home, your lifestyle is sure to slowly but surely take a down turn.

Renovation for increased prosperity

In fact the big economic meltdown which affects millions of people around the world has already started. Since the sub-prime scandal of 2008 in USA, which was followed by the global money and wealth meltdown in that same year, the structure and perspective of the world's rich and prosperous have changed drastically. Those most badly affected by what happened are those still living in Period 7 houses! The mortgage lenders and banks that suffered the most problems, the companies that were the hardest hit are all those who did not transform their living and working energies into Period 8 buildings.

Why was this? Simply because they did not know how to! Thus if you want to benefit from this new Period's energy, which is growing more robust by the day, you should make an effort to change your house or office energy into that of Period 8.

Since Period 8 is still "young," having only started in 2004, and will not end until 2024, many houses in existence have not yet become Period 8 buildings. They cannot become Period 8 buildings unless they have been re-energized with a fairly extensive renovation.

Houses and apartments that were completed after February 4 2004, however, are regarded as Period 8 abodes. These enjoy a robust and fresh energy that translates into good fortune luck.

However, most buildings and houses built before 2004 are Period 7 buildings. They are described in feng shui as having lost most of their chi energy when the period changed in 2004. Old energy gives way to new energy and mankind must revitalize all manmade dwellings to ensure that the chi within them stays in sync with the changing time dimension. The practice of feng shui must thus be kept up to date in terms of the Period changes in chi energy. It is necessary to stay contemporary in feng shui!

Period 8 homes are now much luckier than Period 7 properties. Businesses with Period 8 addresses are more insulated against financial loss than their competitors with a Period 7 address.

Becoming a Period 8 house or office 53

Any building, apartment, or house completed and occupied by human energy after February 4 2004 is considered a Period 8 abode. Such a building enjoys fresh new chi, which benefits its inhabitants by bringing them good yang energy and great vitality.

For a building that was built before this date, it is necessary to revitalize the energy within by significantly renovating its interiors. This cannot be a cosmetic job but must be thorough and quite extensive—often requiring inhabitants to move out while renovations are carried out.

First, all doors and windows should be opened to allow fresh energy to flow into the home. Most importantly there should be a door or window in the northwest sector of the home as this is the path of 8. It is through a northwest opening that fresh new period 8 chi enters any home or office.

Next the main door must be changed. Have a new door made from freshly-cut wood, one that is solid and strong and tough! This signifies mankind energy, the chi of humankind that must be revital-

ized to bring new luck into the home. Merely repainting a tired old door does no good for the energy of the home.

Next change the roof, or for those living in apartments the ceiling, to allow new "heaven energy" to enter the home. If you cannot change all of your roof, then change at least a third of it! Use new tiles because you need some new energy. Again, simply cleaning and repainting the tiles is insufficient to change the energy of your home! You need part of the roof to be opened for new heaven energy to permeate through.

The third thing to replace is your floor. This transforms the Earth energy, and is the most important change to make. Some may be reluctant to change a beautiful marble floor—alas a couple of wealthy families I know who resisted changing for this reason have lost two thirds of their wealth! Change at least a third of your floor so that new Earth chi permeates your home. For those living in apartments, you can consider changing the flooring and carpets of your home.

Revitalize the tien ti ren

Implicit in everything I have suggested about changing your house into a Number 8 home is that your home's tien ti ren energy—heaven, earth and humankind energy—gets revitalized and re-energized. Do this as soon as possible and you will see your luck transform, allowing you and your family to benefit from the chi energy of the current period. This is the most important piece of advice in this entire book!

Changing the flooring in your home will bring in Period 8 energy.

54   The feng shui house chart

Aflying star feng shui house chart has nine grids to represent the nine palaces of a home. There are eight direction sectors on the four sides and there is a center grid, which represents the heart of the home. The numbers in the center of the chart are very important. If they are lucky numbers—if they are 1, 6, 8, or 9—they should be magnified by activating them with noise, lights, or activity; all three represent yang energy! When they are afflictive—if they are 2, 5, 3, or 7—they should be suppressed or locked up, especially when they are 5 or 3. These numbers bring misfortunes and aggravations! It is very important to keep sectors occupied by them very quiet.

Altogether there are 16 charts for all houses of the period of 8, each one based on a house's facing direction. Choose the chart correctly and then analyze their effect on your house by superimposing the chart onto your house floor

plan. If you have more than one level repeat the process by superimposing the same house chart on every level of your home. Do make sure you use a good compass to locate the sectors correctly and have patience learning this method—do not expect to know how to use the charts immediately. Once you get it, however, you will have learnt a very powerful formula of feng shui!

Every house chart shows that there are three numbers in each of the nine sectors, or palaces. The center number of each palace is the Period star number of that sector. So in all the Period 8 charts the center number is 8. Note, however, that it is not the big number that exerts the greater influence. Actually it is the smaller numbers to the right and left of the main number that are the most important from a feng shui perspective.

The Water and Mountain stars

The small number on the right in each palace is the Water star number, which governs everything to do with wealth luck. When the number is a lucky number such as 8, 1, or 6, it suggests good wealth luck for the sector it appears in and when the number is unlucky it means misfortunes associated with your ability to earn or make money. Auspicious Water stars should always be activated by the presence of physical water to enable you to benefit fully from a lucky Water star.

The small number on the left in each palace is the Mountain star number, and the number situated here in every grid gives an indication of the relationship luck of that sector where the number appears. Once again when the number is a lucky number such as 8, 1, or 6, it suggests good health and relationship luck for the sector it appears in and when the number is unlucky it means misfortunes associated with your health and your relationships. Lucky Mountain stars should always be activated by the presence of mountains—either actual mountains, a high wall or some elevated ground. If not then a painting of mountains! This is what enables you to benefit fully from an auspicious Mountain star.

On this Period 8 chart the Period star, 8, is shown in the center of the grid. The two small numbers that go with each big number are the Mountain and Water stars.

The Mountain star is always to the left of the big number. The Water star is to the right of it. Here, both the highlighted stars are 8.

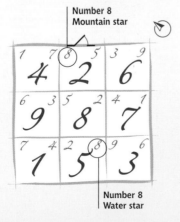

Number 8
Mountain star

Number 8
Water star

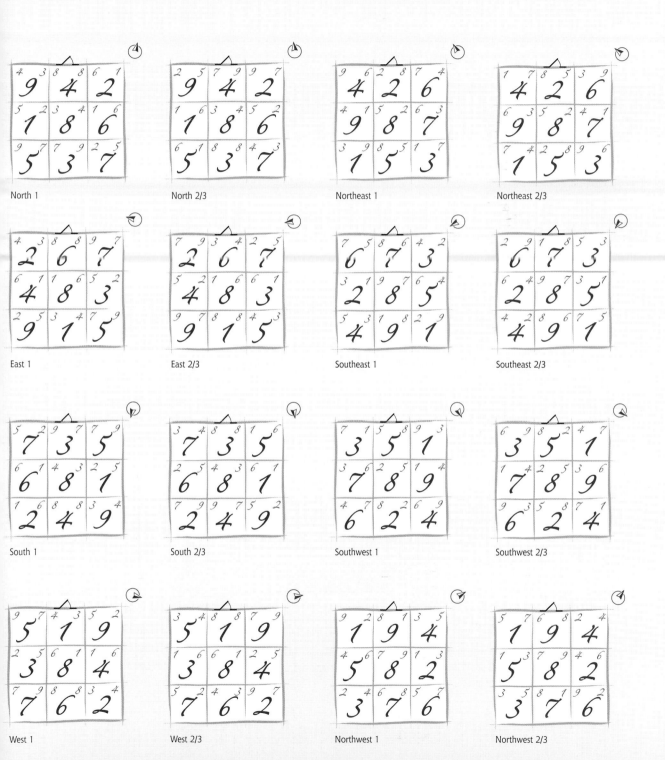

North 1

North 2/3

Northeast 1

Northeast 2/3

East 1

East 2/3

Southeast 1

Southeast 2/3

South 1

South 2/3

Southwest 1

Southwest 2/3

West 1

West 2/3

Northwest 1

Northwest 2/3

55 Numbers in your feng shui chart

Numbers can be yin or yang, active or passive.

Examine the feng shui charts carefully and you will see that each of the numbers 1 to 9 have special meanings and attributes that are different from the meanings assigned to Birth and Name Numbers explained in earlier sections (see Tips 1–24). The numbers in the feng shui flying star charts help us interpret the energy of space, especially as it changes over time. These numbers tell us about the nature of chi energy, luck potential, and impending good or bad news. From this perspective, therefore, it is necessary to know what these numbers mean in a feng shui context.

Numbers in feng shui also have corresponding element associations—each linked to one of Fire, Earth, Metal, Water, or Wood. The element of the number has an impact on the chi of the space they "fly" into from year to year and in different periods. As such the meanings of numbers can change depending where they are placed in the chart and when superimposed onto houses. This is

something master practitioners of feng shui take note of.

Yin and yang

Numbers are also either yin or yang and this creates yet another layer of meaning. When numbers are yang they are active, but when they are yin they are inactive. This is also related to the different strengths of numbers during different time periods, so the meaning of a particular number can have very different emphasis in different periods. The readings and explanations given here are based on the strength of numbers in the current Period of 8.

Numbers also have different meanings depending on whether they signify the Water star, the Mountain star or a time star (annual or monthly). Numbers must be interpreted according to whether they are Period numbers, Water star numbers, or Mountain star numbers.

Numbers can also be Year Numbers or they can be Month Numbers. The meanings of numbers in these house charts reflect the dynamic nature of time, which never stands still. Numbers interpret energy, which changes every moment, each day, and every month.

It is certainly not within the scope of this book to go into the details of how to interpret all the different numbers. For that you will need to sign up for an advanced course in feng shui. For now, however, it is useful and beneficial just to understand the base charts of feng shui that use numbers and to know what the set of three numbers in the charts—the Water star, the Mountain star, and the Period star—means for you. Just determine the correct chart that applies to your home and study their meanings from the meaning of numbers given here.

The secrets of feng shui

In the old days, the practice of time feng shui was a closely guarded secret used only by learned masters. These master practitioners would update the feng shui of their patrons each year to address the annual changes of chi energy, and also attend to the cyclical twenty-year period changes.

Feng shui masters have always used the Lo Pan compass, which associates directions, elements, and formulae.

Meaning of numbers in your feng shui chart 56

There are so many classical texts on the subject of numbers in feng shui that it is impossible to note every nuance of meaning for every single number, or combination of numbers. I believe it is sufficient to take note of the most important meanings of each of the nine numbers. So those wanting to understand the significance of numbers in the feng shui of houses must first note that in Period 8 the dangerous numbers are 5 and 2, The number 7 has also become dangerous, while the number 3 is quarrelsome. These four numbers suggest misfortune and bad luck of some kind. The severity of their effect depends on where they are in the house and what numbers reside along side them in the sector they are placed in.

The lucky numbers 1, 6, and 8

The three lucky individual numbers are 1, 6, and 8; these are described as the white numbers. Of the three numbers 8 is the luckiest and wherever it shows up, it activates the chi of the star it is. Using this guideline feng shui experts are especially keen on the Water star 8 as being a powerful generator of wealth luck when the sector it occupies in the home gets activated or enhanced.

The numbers 1 and 6 are also lucky numbers but these are not given the same level of reverence as 8. Number 1 means the first in the series and also stands for career and income generating potential. The 6 signifies luck from heaven.

The number 9

This is a magnifying number. It multiplies good luck as well as bad luck. On its own it is a good-luck star but its energy has not yet ripened; when it does, after 2024, the number 9 will become amazingly powerful. In Period 8 charts, 9 is to be feared when it strengthens the misfortune stars 2 and 5.

The number 2

This is the illness star in feng shui. It brings sickness and makes residents more vulnerable to common colds, coughs, flu and other viruses. When it is strengthened by 9, or when it occurs in an Earth element sector (such as the northeast or southwest of your house) it becomes extremely dangerous. When it is combined with the misfortune 5 the negative chi generated by the combination becomes incredibly unpleasant.

The number 5

In feng shui, number 5 is known as the wu wang or five yellow. It is considered the most dangerous of the nine numbers and when the annual 5 flies into any sector it brings misfortune, loss, and sickness. In any house chart, 5 should be contained by hanging a six-rod, all-metal wind chime in the afflicted sector. Those made of brass are great but the best are wind chimes made of real gold!

The number 4

This is a good star number. It is also the romantic and literary star bringing extreme good fortune for writers and scholars. Its benefits are enhanced when combined with the number 1, although this combination can sometimes lead to sexual scandals caused by illicit love affairs.

The number 7

This was lucky in the past twenty years but turned unlucky in 2004 when its true nature reverted. In the new Period 8, number 7 brings loss, burglary, and violence. It is not a nice star to have in the bedroom as it causes betrayal and mistrust to set in.

The number 4 is the star of romance and also literature, so is a good omen for writers and lovers!

57 Activating your lucky Water star for wealth luck

The Water stars sits on the right and the Mountain star on the left.

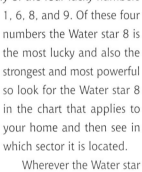

When you read a feng shui house chart, the intention is to activate the three most important types of luck that determine our quality of life. This means concentrating on our wealth, health, and relationship happiness luck. This can be done by looking at the Water stars for wealth luck and the Mountain stars for health and relationship luck.

To attract wealth into the home and to ensure that it continues to stay in the home, lasting through into the next generation, you should look for lucky Water stars; this means Water stars that are represented by any of the four lucky numbers 1, 6, 8, and 9. Of these four numbers the Water star 8 is the most lucky and also the strongest and most powerful so look for the Water star 8 in the chart that applies to your home and then see in which sector it is located.

Wherever the Water star 8 is located you simply must have physical water in the form of a pond, a pool, or a water feature. The nicer the pool or pond is the better and, of course, it should be yang, with movement, life, lights, or all three present. Pools or ponds by themselves may be lucky but they do little for your feng shui unless they are activated through usage and life. This is the reason why the Chinese like to keep fish since this suggests the life force that is so vital to activating for good luck.

The Water star 8 gets energized and will attract wealth chi into the home when there is the presence of physical water, and usually the deeper the water the deeper the wealth luck! Thus the Water star 8 is best activated on landed property. If you live in an apartment, it is a good idea to invest in a good-looking water feature to decorate your living room… but only if it is located in the sector where the Water star 8 is.

In Period 8 charts, the Water star 8 is always located in either the front facing palace or the back sitting palace of the home. This is a very important observation about Period 8 houses and those looking to invest in a new house should really take note of this.

The facing palace is the front middle sector which houses the main door—hence its name. The sitting palace is at the back of the house and this is the center of the back sectors. For this reason I always advise my clients and students to ensure that the middle part of homes is kept clutter free and beautifully decorated with auspicious objects. This adds to the powerful effect of suitably placed water features.

Activate the Water star 8 for luck

The Water star 8 is a lucky star bringing good feng shui when it is in the front facing palace of the house. When the Water star 8 is at the back it is deemed to be reverse water! At the back the Water star 8 is said to be in reverse gear, and it is not as good as if the Water star 8 was at the front.

If you have an odd-shaped house so that the sector that houses the Water star 8 is "missing" you can still activate Water star 9 to energize future prosperity, or Water star 1 for business success. The skill is to locate the good luck Water stars in your home and activate those corners with physical water.

Water in your home or home environs activates the powerful Water star.

Activating your lucky Mountain star for good health and relationship luck 58

Activating the auspicious Water and Mountain star sectors of your house is one of the most powerful ways to activate good feng shui. While Water stars bring wealth luck Mountain stars bring good health and robust happy relationships into your life. Here the word relationship is used in its widest possible context and while the main relationship that a lucky Mountain star blesses is that of the husband and wife, a good Mountain star also benefits relationships between siblings—brothers and sisters—and even between employees and employers.

Any home benefiting from a good Mountain star 8 that is properly energized by the presence of real or "pseudo" mountains is sure to enjoy a life free of aggravations and relationship problems. Everything goes smoothly and there will be little cause for misunderstandings to arise.

The lucky Mountain star 8 gets activated to bring good health to the residents of the home when there is the presence of mountain energy, which can be simulated by pictures of mountains, crystals, and walls made of bricks or concrete. The most auspicious way of benefiting from the lucky Mountain star is the presence of real natural mountains in the extended direction of the sector housing the auspicious Mountain star. Their very presence is what brings amazingly powerful health and relationship luck.

Create your own mountain luck

If you live in a city then big buildings can also be viewed as mountains although, of course, natural mountains are always more powerful than man-made buildings either in a negative or positive way. If you live in an apartment, it is a good idea to invest in a good mountain painting where the

Mountain stars occurring in the back of the home, boost relationship luck. In the house plan below, the Mountain star 8 is in the sitting palace at the back of the house, which is auspicious.

Mountain star 8 resides. This is the best way of activating a good Mountain star.

As with the auspicious Water star 8 in all Period 8 charts, the lucky Mountain star 8 is also always located in either the front facing palace or the back sitting palace of the home. This is a very important observation about Period 8 houses and those looking to invest in a new house should really take note of this. The Mountain star 8 is thus either a lucky Mountain star or a reverse Mountain star. For good feng shui it is better for the Mountain star to be at the back sitting palace of the house where it is deemed to be lucky; when the Mountain star 8 is at the front it is deemed to be reverse mountain! When it is in front the mountain is said to "block" the luck of the house.

The sitting palace is at the back of the house in the center. If you can see mountains from here you will benefit greatly.

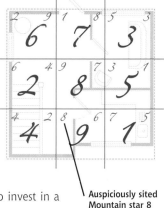

Auspiciously sited Mountain star 8

59 Extraordinary luck of special number combinations

In addition to the meanings of the single individual numbers, it is useful to go a little deeper into the numbers and look out for the auspicious specials. These are unique combinations of numbers that create the potential for residents of houses having them in their feng shui charts to enjoy the most amazingly good feng shui. In fact the main reason for learning feng shui should be to look for "secrets" like these!

These combinations occur rarely—at most in only one or two charts in each period—and in some periods they do not even occur at all. I shall be alerting you to the charts where these combinations occur. If you are building a new house and you can build a house with this kind of chart you should definitely strive to do so.

These specials include two numbers that combine into a "sum-of-ten" in every sector, or three numbers occurring in combinations that represent the "parent string" again in every sector.

Either of these two sets of specials would be considered outstanding feng shui when properly used and activated.

The sum of ten numbers are two-number combinations of 1/9, 2/8, 3/7, 4/6, and 5/5. The way to activate these numbers when they occur is to display auspicious symbols in multiples of ten by having ten dragons, ten crystal balls, and so forth...

The parent string combination are three number combinations made up of numbers 1, 4, and 7; 2, 5, and 8; and 3, 6, and 9. The way to activate them is to keep the home well ventilated, well lit and suffused with sufficient yang chi either by having good noise levels or with the sounds of life always present.

These auspicious specials are said to override any bad numbers that may appear in any sector, and have the power to bring exceptional good fortune, abundance, and wealth. Residents will enjoy excellent descendants luck and amazingly good relationship and mentor luck.

You will find that in Period 8 there are two facing direction house charts that contain the auspicious specials and for this reason alone those of you fortunate enough to have houses that fit these charts should definitely change the period of your house to that of Period 8. If you can successfully change the period of your house, you would then be able to tap these best charts in the Period 8.

Does your home have extraordinary luck?

Charts with these special number combinations occur for houses that have a facing direction of northeast or southwest. For this reason it can categorically be stated that all houses facing or sitting on the SW/NE axis will enjoy tremendous excellent good fortune. It does not matter which of the three sub sectors of this direction your house faces. As long as it faces or sits along this axis direction you will be able to keep the house suffused with yang chi—bringing good health, wealth, and happiness fortune to you.

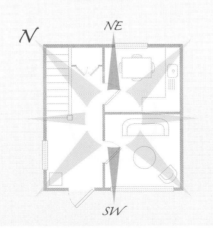

Using the numbers for your house feng shui 60

You need to superimpose the relevant feng shui chart onto the layout of your house to determine which parts of your house benefit from the good numbers. This must be done correctly using a compass to establish the orientation of your home and systematically determining the different sectors that make up the eight compass sector locations of the house.

Step One: Determine which of the Period 8 charts shown earlier apply to your house. I am assuming that everyone reading this book is staying in Period 8 houses. (meaning that your house was built or renovated after February 4 2004) Determine the chart that applies to your home by determining the facing direction of the house. This can be a little tricky but with some practice you should be able to do this. Use your own "feeling" by looking at the house. If you get the facing direction wrong the whole analysis will be flawed!

Step Two: Determine the most meaningful way to superimpose the sector numbers onto the house layout plan. There are different ways to divide the house into sectors that correspond with the eight sectors but you need to do this in order to determine which numbers are influencing the different rooms of the house. Not all feng shui experts agree on the "method" of demarcating sectors in the home. I myself use the room's walls as demarcation markers and I have found this to be a very accurate way of determining the luck according to the numbers of the chart.

With a square house the chart fits easily over the floor plan.

Step Three: Next identify the Period, Mountain and Water stars to get a good idea of where the respective lucky numbers of these stars are located. This will give you a general idea of the "good luck" areas of the house. Remember that lucky Water star numbers are indicated by the numbers 8, 6 or 1 and these bring good wealth luck while the same numbers appearing as Mountain star numbers indicate good relationship and health luck.

Step Four: Look out for the "specials" in the chart that indicate exceptional good luck. These specials include numbers that combine as a "sum-of-ten" or three numbers occurring in combinations that represent the "period or parent string." The key to successful analysis is to be able to read and analyze the numbers as well as to correctly superimpose the numbers onto the different rooms of the house.

The Mountain star 6 and Water star 4 in the far sector make up a sum-of-ten.

Step Five: Study the combination of the Water and Mountain star numbers in each grid and see which star dominates in terms of their elements. This gives you an idea of whether money or relationships will dominate the luck of the residents who reside in that part of the house. Also study the combination of Water with Period and Mountain with Period stars.

The Mountain star 8 is in the facing palace.

61 Misfortune luck numbers

When using feng shui charts always look at the three numbers in each square. All charts are read the same way using the meanings of the numbers to indicate whether they bring good or bad luck; just as there are lucky numbers that suggest good fortune, there are also unlucky numbers that bring different kinds of misfortune.

Misfortune numbers cause a reversal of fortunes, bringing illness, accidents, business setbacks, quarrels, difficulties with the authorities... and many other problems.

Fight misfortune

The list of bad luck manifestations can be long and the results are always aggravating, causing distress and sorrow for those who must endure them. People who have not experienced suffering do not know what it is

like and it is better never to have to go through sufferings of any kind; for these reasons it is beneficial to prevent bad luck from happening to you or your family or to at least reduce its impact. Loss and pain can be reduced to manageable proportions and this is

The rhino and wu lou counteract misfortune.

what Feng Shui numerology, using the flying star method can do with great potency.

The four unlucky numbers to be aware of in the feng shui chart are 2, 3, 7 and 5. Number 2 can bring illness or mental anguish—for how to counteract this, see Tip 74; number 3 brings relationship problems—to counteract these see Tip 71; the number 7 indicates robbery or loss of some kind—to protect against this see Tip 73; number 5 brings misfortune of all kinds—for defensive measures see Tip 76.

62 Being careful about bad numbers

Knowing about charts is one thing but you must also be alert to the dangers of the bad luck numbers, especially when they are hitting your main door or your master bedroom. If your house layout is designed in a way that means these two important sectors of your house are occupied by any of the misfortune numbers then you must put the remedies in place.

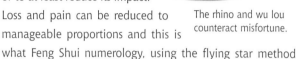

For instance when you know the illness star number 2 is in your bedroom in the feng shui chart, you must take action to control that affliction to avoid getting sick. The best solution is to move to another room, but if this is not possible then make sure the room is painted white,

The pagoda

the lights are kept dim, and there is a metal wu lou (this symbol overcomes the illness star 2) placed inside the room.

Door remedies

If the misfortune star number 5 flies into the sector where your main door is located, you can similarly take action to suppress the affliction. Here the five-element pagoda is the best remedy possible and it is really better to get a brand new one at the start of each year to ensure that its energy stays fresh form year to year.

In feng shui, the principle is to be protected against bad luck numbers at all times, but more so in the parts of the home you occupy the most. As long as bad energy numbers do not hit you, they will not be able to hurt you as badly even though the house itself will slowly lose good chi when troublesome afflictive numbers are not kept under control.

Chinese lunar and solar calendars 63

Not many people realize that the Chinese have two calendars—lunar and solar. The lunar calendar is the one most English-speaking Chinese are familiar with, with the new year falling somewhere in January and February—it is necessary to check the hundred-year calendar to find the start of each new year. This is the calendar that is used in the celebration of Chinese new year; in the determination of one's animal year of birth, in our investigation of our life's destiny analysis, and in determining the heavenly stem and earthly branch elements of our year of birth.

The solar calendar

Flying star feng shui, however, does not use the lunar calendar; instead it uses the lesser-known solar calendar. This is also referred to as the Hsia calendar. It differs from the lunar calendar in that the start of each new year under the solar calendar is February 4 (there is a margin of error of one day in certain years, but it is safe to use this as the changeover date from year to year). This corresponds to the lap chun or start of Spring in each year.

Annual changes in chi energy that affect the time dimension of feng shui are based on the solar calendar to differentiate the timing of years and months, so that those of us who use the Western Gregorian calendar must take note of the solar year and the solar months of the Hsia or solar calendar. When we speak of annual and monthly feng shui charts that lay out the luck of houses from year to year and from month to month, it is necessary to convert Western calendar dates to the equivalent Chinese solar calendar dates.

In each new Chinese solar year, there will be a ruling number, and this number is used to create the annual feng shui chart that reveals the luck of different sectors of the house for that year.

The Chinese usually refer to annual almanacs to determine these all-important Year and Month Numbers but in the tables here I have summarized the ruling numbers for the next 12 years and the ruling numbers for the different months, all based on the solar calendar.

These numbers enable anyone to work out the annual feng shui charts of every year and every month, with the equivalent cut off dates that enable you to convert to a Western calendar. To obtain the feng shui annual chart of any year or month, all you need to do is determine the ruling number of the year or month. This ruling number goes to the center of the chart and all other numbers are filled in, in accordance to the sequential arrangement of the Lo Shu square (see Tips 131–135).

Although the dates may have a variation of plus or minus one day these tables are a summary of the 10,000-year calendar that can be consulted for more accurate analysis of the luck according to different months of the years.

Reigning numbers for solar calendar from 2010 to 2021

Year		Reigning number	Year		Reigning number
2010	tiger	8	2016	monkey	2
2011	rabbit	7	2017	rooster	1
2012	dragon	6	2018	dog	9
2013	snake	5	2019	boar	8
2014	horse	4	2020	rat	7
2015	sheep	3	2021	ox	6

Reigning numbers for solar calendar months in various years

Start of month	Year of rat, rabbit, horse, & rooster	Year of dog, dragon, ox, & sheep	Year of tiger, pig, snake, & monkey
February 4	8	5	2
March 6	7	4	1
April 5	6	3	9
May 6	5	2	8
June 6	4	1	7
July 7	3	9	6
August 8	2	8	5
September 8	1	7	4
October 8	9	6	3
November 7	8	5	2
December 7	7	4	1
January 6	6	3	9

64 Annual change of ruling numbers

Flying star numbers change every twenty-year period, and also annually, so it is important to check annual ruling numbers to maximize your house luck.

The reason why analyzing your annual and monthly feng shui is so important is because everyone must take note of the annual afflictions that are revealed by the annual chart each year. These afflictions can sometimes cause such tremendous bad luck that losses and illness can be fatal and it may be difficult to recover from any severe bad luck experienced.

Depending on what type of affliction it is, and in which sector the affliction hits, sometimes these annual horrors can cause bankruptcy, loss, and even death. How severe they are depends on your personal luck and the strength of your home's chi in any particular year so it is a good idea to also update your astrological readings every year. These are summarized in my annual "Fortune and Feng Shui" books for each of the twelve animal signs.

Subduing annual (and monthly) afflictions is part of the regular updating you need to do to ensure your feng shui stays protective and auspicious. It is foolish to ignore this updating process because it does not require much effort.

Not updating your feng shui each start of the year can easily cause illness, business collapses, a sudden loss of employment, car or other accidents, separations, and divorces. These kinds of sudden misfortunes can be avoided, or at least have their severity reduced, by placing the suggested remedies in place. The process begins by understanding the influence of the annual numbers in the feng shui annual and month charts.

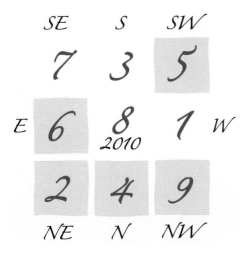

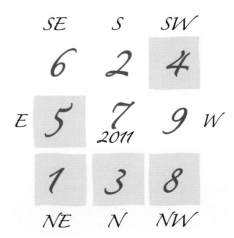

These house charts for 2010 and 2011 show the ruling number 8 for 2010 and number 7 for 2011.

Important annual afflictions 65

Updating your feng shui each year by using the annual chart is an important dimension of feng shui practice. It is truly vital to take note of the annual afflictions and then to suppress their effects with suitable feng shui remedies. The three major annual afflictions are:

- the five yellow, also known as wu wang
- the three killings, also known as sarm sart
- the Grand Duke Jupiter, also known as Tai Sui

Although I usually post annual affliction warnings on my website—www.wofs.com—together with suggested cures at the start of each year, those of you reading this book should be able to work out the afflictions on your own. More important is to take note of the cures needed to overcome these afflictions; although of course the best cure is to avoid them altogether if this is possible.

What to do if your bedroom is afflicted

If your bedroom is afflicted by either the wu wang or the sarm saat it is best to simply move into another room for the year if that is possible. This is because the cures may reduce the effect but when the affliction is strengthened by a sector or the furniture in it without your knowledge, then whatever cures you place may be ineffective.

Furthermore, if either your bedroom or front door is affected by any one of the three afflictions and the month and year numbers there are also inauspicious then the danger gets considerably heightened. The best thing then is to move out of that room for the year when the affliction takes place even if it means sleeping in the living room. If you really cannot do this then you should use a symbolic cure to reduce the affliction's impact. It is hard to completely overcome the annual afflictions but this depends on the cure you use. Also, note

Check out the annual afflictions affecting your bedroom—you may need feng shui remedies to protect your luck.

that sometimes different years require different remedies because the afflictions fly to different parts of the house. Remedies should also not be reused. It is always better to bring in new remedial symbolic cures each year as fresh new energy makes them stronger and more effective.

The sector that houses the main door is the other part of your home that is usually the most vulnerable to the annual afflictions. If one of them hits this sector, the whole house will feel its effect. This means you should always check the annual and monthly stars that fly into the facing palace of the house. If the main door is afflicted it is definitely advisable, if possible, to look for another door to use for the duration of that year. This is because the opening and closing of the door strongly activates the affliction. If using an alternative door is not an option for you, then you are left no other choice but to install special feng shui cures to reduce the effect of the affliction.

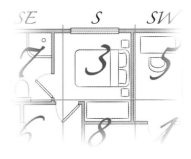

This bedroom is afflicted by the annual 3 star, or three killings. The best remedy is to move out of that room for the remainder of the year.

66 Exhausting the five yellow

The wu wang or five yellow affliction is very harmful and in certain years can cause extreme damage to a family or a company whose home or office is directly hit by it. It is something everyone doing business should be aware of. The five yellow is the number 5 in the annual feng shui chart. Every year it is to your great advantage to find out where the five yellow is located and to apply powerful cures to suppress it.

In 2009 the five yellow was in the north, where it did not wreak as much damage as the previous year when it was in the south; in the north the element of Water is not strong enough to overcome the five yellow but Water does distract it thereby making it less strong. In both instances it was necessary to place the traditional remedy, which is the five-element pagoda.

Reinvigorate with bells and chimes

In 2010 the five yellow misfortune star flies to the southwest where it creates danger to anyone living in this sector. The remedy for 2010 is the five-element bell or five-element pagoda with the ten powerful mantras. In the southwest the five yellow is extremely strong and it is necessary to use strong Metal energy to suppress it.

When the wu wang occupies the sector of the house where the main door is located, it becomes dangerous irrespective of which compass sector this is, mainly because each act of opening and closing the door, or any kind of activity in the place of the wu wang, will energize its bad vibrations causing misfortunes to befall. When disturbed or activated the five yellow always brings calamities, accidents, illness, loss, or a battalion of these troubles. So if your main door is afflicted by the wu wang, you must put the metal five-element pagoda cures there.

The idea is to exhaust the chi energy of the five yellow, and since its element is Earth, Metal energy is needed—so other cures are brass coins and windchimes where the number 6 features strongly. Number 6 is a Metal number so six-rod windchimes or six large coins would work well to control the five yellow. However in the current Period of 8 the best cure is the five-element pagoda. Place a brass or gold-plated five-element pagoda exactly where the five yellow is located in any year to effectively contain its negative misfortune chi.

In 2009 the five yellow was in the north, and moves through the southwest and east sectors in 2010 and 2011.

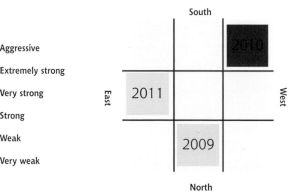

- ■ Aggressive
- ■ Extremely strong
- ■ Very strong
- ■ Strong
- □ Weak
- □ Very weak

Remedies for the five yellow include coins in groups of six and metal six-rod windchimes.

More facts on the five yellow 67

The five yellow occupies 45 degrees of the compass and to find its location in your house you need to use a compass once you have determined its location in the annual chart. Every year ensure that finding the location of the five yellow in your house and then suppressing it is the thing you do before anything else.

It must also be remembered that the five yellow is associated with some feng shui taboos which must be adhered to. These are:

- You must not dig the ground where the five yellow is located in each year. Doing so will cause you to become ill instantly and this may be followed by other misfortunes.
- You must not cut down any trees where the annual five yellow is. Doing so activates the affliction immediately and you either get sick or have an accident. Alternatively, your business will suffer a sudden setback, which could be irreparable.

- You must not disturb that part of the land or house in anyway either with excessive noise, bright lights or activity. Do not keep dogs or pets there as they disturb the five yellow, thereby activating it.
- You must not renovate that part of the house. This involves banging and digging and is definitely not advisable. If you need to do renovations to parts of the house that involve the sector with the five yellow, then make certain you do not start or end the renovation in the place of the five yellow.

When disturbed and activated, the five yellow brings loss of wealth, loss of employment, accidents, injuries and calamities, robbery, and sometimes it can even bring death. The five yellow occurs in the year chart as well as the month star and, when they coincide, anyone residing in that corner of the home will immediately get ill. It is even worse when the five yellow of the year and month also coincide with the five yellow in the feng shui house chart. This is a major indicator of some big misfortune occurring unless there are plenty of powerful antidotes used in the form of the metal five-element pagoda and bell.

Follow the five yellow

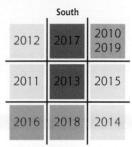

South

2012	2017	2010 2019
2011	2013	2015
2016	2018	2014

North

Year	Position	Strength
2010	Southwest	strong
2011	East	weak
2012	Southeast	weak
2013	Center	very strong
2014	Northwest	weak
2015	West	weak
2016	Northeast	strong
2017	South	very strong
2018	North	strong
2019	Southwest	strong

Digging at the location of the five yellow is believed to cause misfortune.

68   Confronting the three killings

The three killings direction brings three types of misfortunes and it occupies one of the four cardinal sectors—north, south, east, or west—in any given year. So this is an affliction that covers 90 degrees of the compass and from that viewpoint it is terribly dangerous. In 2010, the year of the tiger, the three killings is in the north. This means that during 2010 sitting with the direction north behind you is dangerous. If your back is to the three killings it will harm you so you must turn to face the three killings affliction.

Facing the three killings ensures that you will directly confront it and doing so is the best way to overcome its pernicious effect. When you face it, it will not hurt you, but having it behind you will hurt you a great deal and subject you to three types of misfortune, including the misfortune of being betrayed and cheated. It is always beneficial to sit directly facing the three killings head on.

When you are planning house repairs you must not work in sectors that house the three killings. Thus in 2010 this means not undertaking any renovations in the north of your house. You may, though, undertake renovations in sectors that are opposite the three killings.

The fu dog is a celestial guardian which can help protect against the negative effect of the three killings

Follow the three killings

Follow this guide to locate the place where the three killings flies to each year.

In dog, horse, and tiger years it is in the north (2010)
Antidote: Place three large boulders in the north during these years.

In pig, rabbit, and sheep years it is in the west (2011)
Antidote: Place more bright lights in the west in these years.

In monkey, rat, and dragon years it is in the south (2012)
Antidote: Place a large container of yin (still) water in the south to overcome its effects.

In ox, snake and, rooster years the 3 killings is in the east (2013)
Antidote: Place a curved knife in the East during these years.

In dog, horse, and tiger years it is in the north (2010)

In pig, rabbit, and sheep years, the 3 killings is in the west (2011)

In ox, snake, and rooster years the 3 killings is in the east (2013)

In monkey, rat, and dragon years, it is in the south (2012)

The best remedy for keeping the three killings under control in any year is the placement of the three celestial guardians—the Fu dog (above), the Pi Yao and the Chi lin.

Appeasing the Grand Duke Jupiter 69

His Chinese name is Tai Tsui and the Chinese regard him as the God of the year; his location each year follows the path of the planet Jupiter and for this reason we call his star the Grand Duke Jupiter. It occupies 15 degrees of space on the compass.

Each year it changes location and for those practicing feng shui it is important to note its position each year and then make sure that one does not confront that direction during that year. This means that one should never sit facing the direction of the Grand Duke Jupiter as doing so brings misfortunes and obstacles, so never sign contracts, negotiate a deal, or make important presentations while facing in this direction. No one should face him directly when they sit, work, eat, give a speech, lead an army, or start a campaign… The Grand Duke can cause havoc when you confront him, and then you could well feel the full impact of his wrath.

The Grand Duke of each year is different and exhibits different characteristics, bringing different kinds of afflictive effects when confronted or disturbed. In some years the effects are fiercer than in others and usually the kind of Grand Duke in each year is revealed in an annual Chinese almanac. Once you know where the Tai Tsui is located, you must make certain you do not incur his wrath by sitting in a direction that directly confronts his direction. If you face his direction it is construed as confronting him, something you simply must not do.

The Grand Duke always resides in the place that corresponds to the animal sign of that year, and he occupies only fifteen degrees of the compass.

In any given year usually the animal sign that is directly opposite to his location is said to be clashing with him and this brings hostile and unfortunate luck to those born under that sign. In the year of the tiger, for instance, the animal sign of the monkey clashes with the Tai Tsui so those born in the

The pi yao placed outside the home helps protect against the Grand Duke.

year of the monkey must make every effort to appease the Grand Duke.

Traditionalists place the pi yao (also known as the pi kan or pi xie) inside the home in the direction of the Tai Tsui. This is believed to be a very effective cure to ensure that he is not offended. Having this protector outside the home is a popular way to create powerful feng shui protection.

My advice is to always place a pi yao image in the home since this is one of the most auspicious celestial creatures anyway. In this way one never has to worry about offending the Grand Duke in any year as the presence of the pi yao image in the home is usually sufficient to appease this affliction.

If you go to Shanghai you can see giant images of the pi yao displayed outside the Shanghai Museum and these are copies of a statue from the Tang period. In some of the old books I consulted this creature is billed as the pi xie, and described as a special celestial creature that was used during the Tang and earlier dynasties as guardians to ward off ill luck brought by changes in time periods.

There are different postures of this creature and you can display them in any style you wish. Just a single one is said to be sufficient to appease the Tai Tsui of each year.

Whenever possible, never sit facing the Grand Duke Jupiter.

70 Enhancing your annual wealth luck

Check out the annual and Period 8 charts for your home to see how your wealth luck might be affected.

When you become familiar with the use of numerology in enhancing your feng shui, you will come to see the great value of updating your space chi each year. This is because the ancient masters of feng shui used numbers, and combinations of numbers, to codify the quality, timing, and occurrence of luck.

Thus in time dimension feng shui it is beneficial to first look at the numbers in the feng shui chart that apply to your house and then to also look at the annual chart numbers. There are therefore two sets of numbers to study.

This also means that each of the eight compass sectors of any house is affected not only by the Period of 8 energy as shown in the feng shui house chart, but also by the annual chi energy of any particular year as shown by the annual feng shui chart. How the numbers interact offers clues to the strength or weakness of the numbers, in turn affecting the luck they bring. This applies to both good luck and bad luck numbers.

The position of the number 8 over the next ten years:

South

2018	2014	2016
2017	2010 2019	2012
2013	2015	2011

North

Year	Position	Strength
In 2010	Center	very strong
In 2011	Northwest	weak
In 2012	West	very weak
In 2013	Northeast	strong
In 2014	South	very strong
In 2015	North	strong
In 2016	Southwest	very strong
In 2017	East	very weak
In 2018	Southeast	very weak
In 2019	Center	very strong

Note that when the strength of 8 is weak its wealth-bringing potential gets weakened but when it is strong it brings abundance and prosperity in big measure.

Annual enhancements for wealth

To maintain the prosperity luck of your home, it is a good idea at the start of each new year to examine the feng shui chart of the coming year in detail, and to look where the superb number 8 is located for that year. This indicates that this sector is the wealth-bringing sector and direction for that year. For example in the year 2010 the number 8 will be in the center of the chart so this indicates that good wealth luck is in the center of all built-up areas. The center takes on great significance and here you should place an auspicious wealth-bringing symbol, such as the three-legged toad or the dragon tortoise sitting on a bed of coins or ingots. You can also make a wealth bowl filled with real money and faux ingots and coins. Display these auspicious wealth-attracting decorative symbols to suggest prosperity and abundance in the center of the house in 2010.

The idea is to make full use of the wealth-enhancing powers of the number 8 each year because it is during the current Period of 8 that this number's chi energy is particularly strong. The number 8 is also an Earth number so placing the figure of 8 made of crystal with real gold flecks inside the 8 is an excellent enhancer for all homes. The important thing is to keep track of the flight path of the number 8 as it flies around the house from year to year.

Safeguarding your annual relationship luck   71

It is also absolutely vital to safeguard your relationships luck every year. This requires you to look for the quarrelsome star number of 3 in the annual feng shui chart. This number 3 star brings havoc and its strength in its place as an annual star number can cause it to wreak havoc in the relationships of people who get hit by it, unless it is strongly suppressed.

The number 3 is a Wood element number that is made stronger by the presence of Water, so, when it flies into the North sector or is in a part of the home where there is the presence of physical water such as a pond or water feature, the fearsome vibes of the number 3 star become more dangerous. That is when this number will not just cause misunderstandings and heated words in the home, it could also lead to violence, and worse it can cause members of the household, especially those staying in rooms where the number 3 star resides in that year, to get into trouble with the law or even to turn violent because it may prevent them controlling their anger.

The number 3 star is usually the cause of court cases being taken out against you and for you being targeted by bullies at school or at the work place. In short the consequences brought by the number 3 star can be hurt and anger in your relationships.

Fight hostility and unreasonableness

When you find yourself feeling hostile, unreasonable, or just plain aggravating you must instantly suspect that it is due to you being hit by the number 3 star. You will notice that in the lives of celebrities, —such as Paris Hilton, Michael Jackson, and Britney Spears, for instance—in the years when they kept getting into trouble with the law or being involved in one court case after another, it was because they were hit by the annual 3 star in their homes during that year!

So do make the effort to find out where the 3 star is each year and then suppress its negative effects with powerful Fire and Metal energy. The best remedies against the 3 star are the flaming sword—a golden sword surrounded by an aura of red flames—or a fire ball, also a golden sphere with symbolic flames. Fire-element energy is a powerful remedy to control the 3 star. Sometimes I have even recommended that one entire wall of the afflicted space be painted red to suppress its bad vibes.

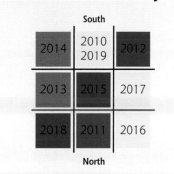

The position of the number 3 star for the next ten years.

	South	
2014	2010 2019	2012
2013	2015	2017
2018	2011	2016
	North	

Year	Position	Strength
2010	South	very weak
2011	North	extremely strong
2012	Southwest	aggressive
2013	East	very strong
2014	Southeast	very strong
2015	Center	aggressive
2016	Northwest	very weak
2017	West	very weak
2018	Northeast	aggressive
2019	South	very weak

Place more remedies to counter the 3 in years when its energy is very strong.

Painting one whole wall of the afflicted space red will suppress its bad vibes.

72 Improving family and marriage luck each year

It is the number 4 star that affects the luck of family and marriage each year. This is a number that is generally associated with the quality of relationships between lovers, romantic partners, and also between spouses in a marriage—some feng shui masters refer to the number 4 as the peach blossom star that brings the romance that leads to marriage. The number 4 does not bring bad luck or death in the context of time formula feng shui; instead it brings a kind of loving energy that tends to bring marriages closer.

The peach blossom star is the number that denotes romance, marriage, and relationship luck.

Dangers occur when it is being afflicted by the presence of too much water. In fact when the number 4 encounters too much water it can cause scandals of a sexual nature and allow infidelity to arise. Remember it is not the presence of the Water element per se that hurts the 4 star, but only too much water— such as a very big aquarium in a very small room—where the number 4 is located in the annual chart. In fact if you are not careful about safeguarding your marriage this way, it can happen that when the 4 flies into a sector of the home that houses your aquarium, you might find the marriage being split apart because of the presence of a scheming outsider! I have seen this happen on several occasions to marriages I had thought were so strong that nothing could tear the couples apart!

Better than Water, a way to stimulate the good energy of the number 4 star is to look for peonies—whether fresh or fake. When you display red or pink peonies in the home it not only brings excellent energies that stimulates the marriage in a positive way but it also enhances the power of the number 4 star to revitalize the romance factor in your relationship. If you cannot find peonies then look for red or pink roses but do remove the thorns! When the thorns are left intact—especially on those amazingly beautiful tea roses of England—instead of bringing romance they bring problems into the relationship as thorns create secret poison arrows.

The position of the number 4 peach blossom star for the next ten years.

Year	Position	Strength
2010	North	very strong
2011	Southwest	very aggressive
2012	East	very strong
2013	Southeast	very strong
2014	Center	aggressive
2015	Northwest	very weak
2016	West	very weak
2017	Northeast	aggressive
2018	South	weak
2019	North	very strong

South

2013	2018	2011
2012	2014	2016
2017	2010 2019	2015

North

Updating to protect your lifestyle   73

One of the key things everyone should take note of is the safety and security of your present way of life. We can call this protecting your assets, your money, your valuables and most of all your lifestyle. This requires you to watch against getting robbed and being burgled of things that belong to you... This usually refers to physical things of course, but in feng shui when we say being robbed of something that is rightfully yours it can also refer to your position, your job, your good name   intangible things like this that mean as much as physical possessions.

To guard against something unfortunate like this happening to you or any members of your family, it is a good idea to update the annual feng shui of your home by looking out for the misfortune star that brings robbery and burglary luck. This is the annual number 7 star that belongs to the element of Metal but is also colored red. For this reason the number 7 is usually also associated with blood—or violence—that is the result of metal forces: guns, knives, swords! The number 7 is thus a number that has extremely unpleasant connotations, bringing with it the negative luck of having someone steal from you or cheat you.

The remedies are a rhinoceros or an elephant with its trunk up, preferably in blue but also powerful when made as a brass image. These two creatures symbolically keep people with bad intentions from reaching you. You will be protected from burglars and cheats, unsavory and dishonest people, when you keep the annual 7 star suppressed. The presence of Water element energy is also excellent for suppressing the ill effects of 7 in house feng shui. One other powerful cure is the 6-tusk Elephant and the source of this comes from an old legend which ascribes magical powers to the 6-tusk elephant.

The position of the number 7 star for the next ten years.

To protect yourself from the 7 star, remember to put your remedies in place before the start of the Chinese solar year.

South

2010	2015	2017
2019	2011	2013
2014	2016	2012

North

Year	Position	Strength
2010	Southeast	very strong.
2011	Center	very dangerous
2012	Northwest	very strong
2013	West	very strong
2014	Northeast	strong
2015	South	very weak
2016	North	very weak
2017	Southwest	very weak
2018	East	very strong
2019	Southeast	very strong

A blue elephant with its trunk raised protects you from others' bad influences.

74 Guarding your health luck every year

Another specific kind of luck to take care of each year is your health luck. To stay healthy and strong, it is vital that the home is always kept clutter-free with stale corners not allowed to develop—these cause yin spirit formation within homes that can be quite dangerous; they can often be the feng shui cause for severe or fatal sickness to hit one of the residents whose personal chi energy level for that year is low. Note that it is extremely helpful to know where you stand in the personal chi energy level stakes each year and this varies from person to person based on your animal sign and the element of your heavenly stem during the year in which you were born.

Your vitality determines how vulnerable you are to bad illness feng shui and to the bad illness star numbers that fly into your room. There are ways to strengthen one's personal chi energy and this varies from person to person—it is what makes using feng shui complete!

The position of the number 2 illness star for the next ten years.

Year	Position	Strength
2010	Northeast	strong
2011	South	very strong
2012	North	strong
2013	Southwest	very strong
2014	East	weak
2015	Southeast	weak
2016	Center	very strong
2017	Northwest	weak
2018	West	weak
2019	Northeast	strong

	South	
2015	2011	2013
2014	2016	2018
2010 2019	2012	2017
	North	

As with all annual stars it is necessary to know where the illness star 2 resides each year. In some years it will be weak but it can also become extremely dangerous. The years when it is strong are the ones when there will be epidemics and different kinds of illnesses causing distress and fear throughout the world to those who do not allay its power.

75 The dangerous combination of 2 and 3

There are three very dangerous combinations of numbers: the first of which is 2 and 3. By itself the number 2 stands for illness, either physical or mental; while 3 on its own stands for hostility and quarrels leading to violence. These meanings are the same whether the numbers appear as Water or Mountain stars in the feng shui chart or as annual numbers in the annual feng shui chart. However, when they occur together—for instance as the Water and Mountain star within the same grid—the combination becomes an explosive indication suggesting misunderstanding or hostility of such severity it can lead to fatal illness. The 2/3 combination can also occur as an annual star number combining with either the Mountain or Water star. When this happens the negative effect is a lot stronger simply because annual stars usually have great strength. Thus, in examining the annual feng shui chart each year, it is a good idea to place all of the numbers 1 through to 9 onto your house chart to see whether there are 2/3 or 3/2 combinations occurring on it.

If such a combination gets created in any year it is vital to place gold and Fire element as cures to subdue its power. This means placing yin Metal and yin Fire element energy (as opposed to yang Metal and Fire). It is necessary for the yin aspect of the two curative elements to be used rather than the yang aspect—the reason for this is that yang forces disturb the 3, making it even more dangerous.

Protecting against reversals in fortune 76

The most dangerous star number is the wu wang or the five yellow, especially when it occurs as the number 5 in the annual feng shui charts. It is imperative to analyze these charts every new year because they enable us to take a defensive posture against identified star numbers that bring troublesome luck. Whatever misfortune luck may be lurking in the home without our knowing must always be flushed out and suppressed because these are like secret poison arrows that cause killing chi energy to bring bad luck.

Updating one's feng shui every year is the core presentation I make at my new year feng shui updating "extravaganzas" when I explain all the important changes that will happen with the advent of the new year. This is always when I offer a very comprehensive outline of what everyone can expect in the new year both at a personal level and also for the rest of the world.

The brass bell is one of the most common cures for the wu wang, or five yellow.

Annual updating

I consider the process of annual updating of the energies around the home to be one of the most important aspects of feng shui practice especially if you are committed to getting the most out of this living skill. It is by constantly updating our personal and home feng shui that we stay protected against misfortunes and well-insulated from the negative manifestations of poor luck. Of the whole lot of negative star numbers, it is the five yellow that one should fear the most. This number serious brings misfortunes each year; and in years when its energy is very high, it is wise to take the warning seriously and not run the risk of falling victim to this star number.

The best cures to be placed where the 5 star is each year will be either the all-metal brass bell or the five-element pagoda with the chien trigram, as well as powerful amulet mantras. This is the best antidote for the 5 misfortune star.

Checking annual updates can help keep your luck flowing in the right direction.

77 The misfortune combination of 2 and 5

The second extremely negative combination of feng shui numbers is the 2/5 or 5/2 combinations which can be exceedingly dangerous. Here either the misfortune star 5 star can combine with the annual illness star to bring major setbacks and obstacles or the illness star 2 can combine with the annual misfortune star 5 in the feng shui chart. The combination of 2 and 5 is very powerful because they are both Earth numbers, which allows them to give strength to each other.

Cures such as the tortoise and coins, along with five-element pagodas and bells (see Tips 37 and 94), are great remedies for the 2/5 or 5/2 combination; but in some circumstances remedies may not be enough, and it is better to vacate an afflicted room.

If your main door or the bedroom you occupy has this sort of numbers combination I would strongly advise you to move out of the room temporarily, or, if you cannot, then to place powerful Metal cures inside the room to exhaust both star numbers. Unless you are diligent about placing remedies to counter this combination the chances of you being hit by a major setback, or by a serious illness that puts you out of action is quite real. In this sort of situation prevention is always much better than cure.

Don't let illness and misfortune combine

Feng shui masters always look for the feng shui chart that applies to a particular house and they will always look at where the misfortune star 5 is, whether as the Water or Mountain star. Next they look at the annual placement of the illness star. Once they locate a sector where both numbers occur together, this instantly rings bells in their head and they will then ensure that suitable cures are installed. It is for this reason that I am such a believer in symbolism because I have discovered form experience that diagnosing the problems in feng shui is only the first part of the practice. The second more important step is to place the remedies, and even these have to be researched because they not only have symbolic requirements, their size, shape, and the material they are made of are also important to their effectiveness.

Excellent remedies for the 2/5 combinations are five-element bells, pagodas, and whirling wu lou cures, and the universal tortoise—but they must be made of metal: brass is best. Metal mirror cures are excellent and they, too, must be made of brass. Just hang them in the sector of the room or house afflicted by the numbers and the affliction will lose strength.

The tortoise and coins

Violence and robbery brought by the 5 and 7 combination

78

Numbers in your charts also assist you in safeguarding your home and workplace from getting burgled, especially the kind of burglary that also brings violence and the shedding of blood with a metal instrument, a gun, or knives. People often ask me if it is possible to feng shui one's house to be protected against burglary and I always say, "Yes!" It can, though, be hard to give a straightforward answer or an instant solution.

It is necessary first to determine whether the house has the kind of negative feng shui that attracts thieves and robbers. Once you have determined that there might be some kind of burglary potential caused by the presence of the 7 star combined with the 5 star, then it is time to place the cures. In the feng shui chart the number 7 is the main number you need to be afraid when it comes to break-ins or falling victim to dangerous criminals, especially when the 7 in the house chart combines with annual 5 or the 5 star in the house chart combines with the annual 7. Both combinations are equally potent.

If your home has this dangerous indication—remember that you really have to do a little bit of work first to determine the chart that applies to your house and then check against the annual chart—the best cure is to place a blue rhinoceros, or alternatively a blue elephant, near the entrance to the home. Water energy near your main door is also an excellent deterrent against burglars.

It is a good idea to renew the cure each new year as this strengthens the protection. I know this may seem very troublesome but it is always beneficial to be as vigilant as possible. Once your cures are in place, however, you can sleep soundly in your bed with no worry.

Burglary
7
NORTH

Although the number 7 burglary star brings violence to the affected location it can be overcome with relatively simple cures—the elephant and the blue rhinoceros.

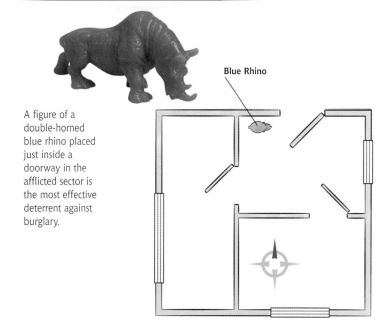

Blue Rhino

A figure of a double-horned blue rhino placed just inside a doorway in the afflicted sector is the most effective deterrent against burglary.

A small water feature inside a home, preferably near a door, also protects against violence and robbery.

79 Combination bringing danger to the women of the household

It is always important to look at the numbers that appear in the southwest and west sectors of any home. Use a compass to find these locations in your home and first see what rooms lie in the southwest. If the main door or the main bedroom is located here, then it has become even more important to protect this sector.

The southwest symbolizes the luck and well-being of the older women in a household—the mother, grandmother, even the aunties too. The southwest sector of any home governs the luck—especially of the mother—so when misfortune numbers fly here, whether as a feng shui chart Mountain star number or as an annual star number, the matriarch's luck tends to get adversely afflicted.

The misfortune numbers are 5—which brings accidents, loss, and illness—the sickness star 2, the quarrelsome star 3—which brings aggravations of the worse kind—and, of course, the burglary and violence star 7. The cures for these numeral afflictions have been dealt with earlier (see Tips 76, 74, 71 and 73).

If you want to get the best from your feng shui practice (without having to resort to expensive consultants) then take a bit of trouble and analyze your relevant house feng shui chart to track down any bad luck numbers. Then suppress these negative numbers with feng shui remedies, and you should be fine.

Also, look after the west sector of your home because this is the part of the house that signifies the young girls of the family. These are your daughters so do look at the numbers that occur here as well, and place any remedies that are needed to protect them.

80 Numbers bringing danger to young children

The same numbers always bring danger and misfortune and we know already that these numbers are 2, 5, 3, and 7—basically these are the numbers associated with intangible energies that are invisible but afflicted. The important thing is to find out where they are located in any chart—that is, in which compass direction—and then use a method of superimposing the chart onto a layout plan of the house to see which important room and which part of the house is hit by the bad numbers.

This actually is the core essence of time dimension feng shui—part of the flying star school that is not just accurate but also extremely timely in offering warning signals of extreme misfortune. This is the great value of this method of feng shui because it uses numbers to code the good and bad effects of time feng shui.

Small, brass pagodas suppress negative energy and are thought to help keep children safe.

To find out if the young children in your household are at risk in any way look carefully at the numbers that fly into the west sector of the home. If there are any children's bedrooms located in this sector note that the danger signs are the Earth stars 5 and 2, though sometimes the presence of the number 4 star can also be a threat to their well-being.

Should you detect any of the negative numbers in this sector you must place the remedies required to suppress whatever number is present. The Earth numbers 5 and 2 are suppressed with Metal cures—wu lous, pagodas, bells, and other esoteric remedies. Always remember that if you want to have continuous protection in the home to safeguard the children of the home, then placing three metal pagodas is an all-time cure. These should be made of metal preferably brass.

Threats to young men and sons 81

When the east and northeast sides of the home are under threat from the negative numbers, the ill effects ripen on the young men or the sons in the family. The east side of the home always governs the luck of the eldest son of the family—his success potential, his health and his success in the classroom and in the sports field. The better the numbers are in the east side of the home, the more the son benefits—and in the Chinese scheme of things, the eldest son is an important member of the household because he is expected to carry on the family name with honor and with success.

The northeast generally stands for the luck of all the sons of the family and in fact the world is currently in the period of the northeast so this is a time that favors the young men of the world. Inside the home, the northeast sector is especially important during the current twenty-year period

that ends in 2024, so it is important to ensure that if there are any bad numbers in the northeast they are properly subdued and kept under control. For instance, if the numbers 5 and 2 are here, unless these are subdued with powerful Metal energy—bells and pagodas made in brass or other metal, and better yet if they contain engraved powerful amulet words or mantras—they will bring grave misfortunes and extreme bad luck to the young men of the family.

Working with remedies

In feng shui knowing the exact nature and kind of remedy is often even more powerful than knowing what is wrong. So the diagnostic aspect of practicing feng shui must be matched with knowledge of remedies for afflictions. These days with the Internet, I can now make everything available to everyone—at the click of a mouse! It is a manifestation of my good feng shui that I am now able to do this.

Check out the northeast sector of your home, as this influences the young men in the family.

82 Danger to the family patriarch

Danger to the father figure, husband, or the patriarch of the household arises when the numbers in the northwest sector of the house or the living room are the afflictive negative numbers. In fact one of the most important aspects of designing the feng shui of any home is to always to pay particular attention to the northwest corner. This is the part of the house that signifies the energy of the father figure. When this corner is missing it actually means that the father figure is missing from the household—either he works away a lot, he has extensive outside interests, or he just does not exist.

Missing corners spell danger

Single women living alone and who have the northwest corner missing will find it hard to find a husband, and those who are married will find that over time the husband seems to be spending less and less time at home, either because he works

Suppressing the danger

When the northwest corner of the home is afflicted by negative numbers this signifies some kind of danger to the father figure so it is vital to suppress the numbers by using the appropriate cure.

Metal wu lou

- Metal pagodas and bells counter the 5
- Metal wu lous suppress the illness star 2
- The red fireball subdues the hostile 3
- The blue rhino or elephant presses down on the burglary star 7

If your home has a northwest sector, and it is not missing due to an uneven house shape, then relationships with men are favored.

late, is away a lot, or travels a great deal in his job... Whether the reason for being away from the home is legitimate or not, the end result is that the house will miss the father figure, so if this is something that sounds like your problem then you will need to do something to correct your missing northwest corner.

Newly married couples moving into a home where the northwest is missing will find the marriage difficult from the start, with the husband staying away from home more than is usual. If a family moves into a new home with the northwest missing this will mean that there will be grave danger to the family, with the father figure eventually staying home less and less...

If it is not possible to suppress the bad numbers in the northwest it is imperative that this corner should not be the site for the master bedroom or the main door! Locate harmless rooms here and any negative afflictions caused by bad luck star numbers can be minimalized.

Activating the wealth-bringing potential of 2   83

One of my favorite recommendations over the past couple of years has been to urge everyone to activate the power of the Period of 8's indirect spirit, which is to activate the number 2 in the southwest sector with physical water.

By placing Water in the southwest we are energizing the power of the sum-of-ten for the current period—that is 2 + 8 (the current period number) = 10—so here with Water in the southwest and mountain spirit in the northeast, we are energizing the sum-of-ten. This sum-of-ten combination is a special wealth-bringer that is highly revered by Taoist feng shui masters. Those who are familiar with the more profound meanings of the formulas of feng shui always focus on activating the sum-of-ten whenever it occurs. In this case we can place water in the southwest sector irrespective of the numbers located there.

Everyone benefits from the presence of water in the southwest. It brings great prosperity luck during this period so those living on landed property should seriously consider having a pond of at least three feet deep, and those wanting to activate their apartment or office can perhaps look for a small water feature, ensuring that the water flows through it both day and night! A decorative aquarium is excellent for energizing the southwest.

Water in the southwest brings wealth.

Strengthening relationship luck   84

You should also activate the northeast to bring the luck of good health and relationships. This is a powerful sector in the current period because we are going through the Period of 8, the number of the northeast. This sector also symbolizes the luck of the young man, so any negative numbers here need to be subdued using element cures.

Having said this, however, irrespective of the numbers here, it is important to energize the northeast simply because it is so powerful at the moment. When it is afflicted it causes problems to surface in your relationships but, conversely, in the current period the northeast is also very strong so good numbers usually have added strength. Why? Because the northeast sector is known as the direct spirit of the period. When the northeast of your house enjoys good feng shui brought by good-fortune numbers such as 1, 6, or 8, then the household enjoys great health and relationships with each other and with outsiders. To strengthen the good luck numbers, display a sizeable crystal geode to signify the mountain—and wait for some amazing good fortune.

If you can do this it will be authentic feng shui at its best. In fact, if you can find some kind of natural stone and have it chiseled to look like three peaks then placing this in the northeast will bring good fortune, benefiting not just the current generation but the next as well.

Boosting the northeast with a crystal supports relationships.

Your eight directions number

Everyone has a personal auspicious direction that can be discovered by finding your Kua Number. By incorporating the positive aspects of this direction into home and lifestyle you can add even more benefit. Discover your lucky and unlucky colors and elements and how your Kua Number can help you select your home and how you use its rooms.

Your eight direction, or Kua Number   85

Each of us has a set of eight directions—four of which are auspicious and four are inauspicious—that is based on the eight direction numbers. The number that is assigned to each individual using this formula is known as a Kua Number and, based on these Kua Numbers, individual auspicious and inauspicious directions and locations can be identified and used to improve our personal feng shui. This is based on a potent formula that divides people into west and east groups with corresponding west or east group lucky and unlucky directions and locations.

I have discovered in over 30 years of feng shui practice that this personalized method is probably the easiest way to use compass feng shui because all you need to compute your Kua Number and find your auspicious and inauspicious directions are your date of birth and your gender. Once you know what your lucky and unlucky directions are all you need is a compass to help you orientate yourself to your lucky direction.

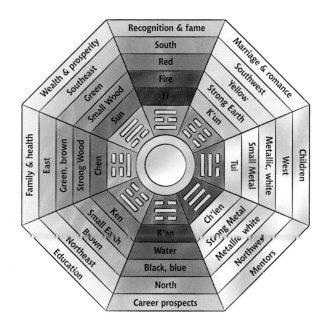

The eight-sided Pa Kua shows the element, color, and trigram associated with each of the eight directions.

Calculating your Kua Number:

Using your Chinese calendar year of birth by using February 4 as new year's day, determine your year of birth, adding the last two digits together. Keep adding the digits until you get a single digit number. Then:

For Men, deduct this number from 10. The result is your **Kua Number**.

For women, add this number to 5. The result is your **Kua Number**.

If you get two digits, keep adding until you reduce it to one digit—if you get the number 10 then $1+0=1$; and if you get the number 14 then $1+4=5$.

Example date of birth: March 6 1956
To determine the Kua Number:
  $5+6=11$, then
  $1+1=2$, then
for men: $10-2=8$ (deducted from 10)
for women: $2+5=7$ (added to five)

Example date of birth: January 3 1962
Because the date of birth is before the lunar new year, we need to deduct 1 from the year so instead of 1962, we will assume that the year of birth is 1961. Thus the Kua Number is $6+1=7$
For men $10-7=3$ (deducted from 10)
For women $7+5=9$ (added to five)

For those born after the year 2000, men will need to deduct from 9 instead of 10 and for girls you will need to add 6 instead of 5.

Once you know your Kua Number all you need to do is refer to the table of auspicious and inauspicious directions.

86 East- and west-group numbers and directions

Depending on your Kua Number you will belong to either the east or the west group of directions; those who belong to the west group benefit from the west group directions and would also benefit from living in west group houses. As such, this method is sometimes known as the "east group, west group" method of demarcating houses and people. Those belonging to the west group will find that they are more compatible with other west group people and that the west-group directions are lucky for them. Meanwhile east-group people will find east-group directions to be lucky for them while west-group directions are not.

The east group

Those whose Kua Numbers are 1, 3, 4, and 9 belong in the east group of directions. All of these—east, southeast, north, and south—are lucky for them. If you are an east-group person note that it will benefit you to live in an east-group house and this means all houses that are deemed to be sitting on east-group directions. These, including houses that face north or south, described as the

Kua Numbers relate to the direction of a house.

east-group axis directions, are excellent for those belonging to the east group because both the sitting and facing directions of the house bring luck to the east-group person.

The west group

Those whose Kua Numbers are 2, 5, 6, 7, and 8 match west-group directions—west, northeast, northwest and southwest—all of which are lucky for these people. If you are a west-group person note that it will benefit you to live in a house that is deemed to be sitting on west-group direction. Houses that face northeast or southwest are described as sitting along the west-group axis. These are deemed to be excellent for those belonging to the west group. As a special note, also remember that in the current Period of 8 all houses that sit along the northeast–southwest axis are especially lucky.

The east group's beneficial directions are shown in yellow, the west group's in blue. The most beneficial axis for the east group is north–south (both east-group directions) while the most auspicious west-group axis is southwest–northeast.

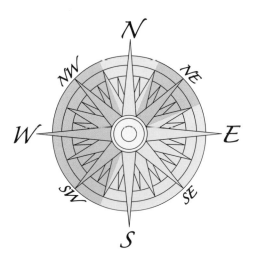

Four kinds of auspicious directions 87

The four directions deemed lucky for people from either the east or west groups can be further fine-tuned into four types of good-fortune directions so that there will be one direction that brings success, one that brings love and romance, one that brings good health, and one that brings personal growth and development. So, depending on what kind of good luck you need or want at any moment in time, you can use a compass to swivel your personal facing direction to capture the energy of the luck you want.

The four kinds of auspicious directions

1. Success—also known as your sheng chi. This direction brings success in competitions, wealth and prosperity luck, as well as very auspicious opportunities for growth and upward mobility. It is the direction to use when you are working or doing business.

2. Love and Romance—also known as the Family and Marriage direction. In Chinese it is known as nien yen and also covers children and descendants luck. Sleep with your head pointing in this direction if you want to enhance your chances of getting married, of having a baby, of improving your love life, or generally improving the harmony of relationships within a family. It is also effective for making difficult children easier to control and more obedient.

3. Health and Longevity—also known as the doctor from heaven, or tien yi in Chinese;

this personalized direction is excellent for those who are older or are generally frail, either recovering from an illness or feeling weak. It is also a direction that protects one against premature death and is able to overcome illness chi brought by changing annual patterns of energy.

4. Personal Growth—also known as fu wei in Chinese. This direction benefits those who are still at school or in college as it is especially good at increasing your knowledge and wisdom. This is a direction that will be the most suitable for those taking examinations, doing their homework, and for those who are spiritually inclined for doing their meditations.

Discover your auspicious directions

It is a good idea to commit these lucky personalized directions to memory as this is one of the easiest ways to practice authentic compass formula feng shui and get results quickly. If you do nothing else save tap into your lucky directions, you will instantly enjoy excellent feng shui. Thus when orientating your sitting and sleeping directions, you must memorize what your personal success (sheng chi) direction is. Refer to the table below and memorize the specific direction that is good for you. Then try as far as possible to always sit directly facing the direction that brings you the kind of luck you want. Thus if wealth and success is what you want then go for the sheng chi direction; and if health is what is important for you, tap the tien yi or doctor from heaven direction and so on.

Your Kua Number	1	2	3	4	5*	6	7	8	9
AUSPICIOUS DIRECTIONS									
Your sheng chi (success direction)	SE	NE	S	N	NE SW	W	NW	SW	E
Your nien yen (romance direction)	S	NW	SE	E	NW W	SW	NE	W	N
Your tien yi (health direction)	E	W	N	S	W NW	NE	SW	NW	SE
Your fu wei (personal development direction)	N	SW	E	SE	SW NE	NW	W	NE	S
East or west group person?	E	W	E	E	W	W	W	W	E

* Kua Number 5, the top numbers are for men, and those below are for women

88 Four levels of bad luck in directions

In the same way that you can fine tune your good luck directions, it is also possible to be very specific about the different effects of the four unlucky directions and these have an element of severity in the kinds of bad luck the direction brings to different people. You have already noted the auspicious directions, so to discover how the bad luck directions play out for you check the table below, Now let's take a look at the four types of bad luck direction in detail. They are:

The four kinds of inauspicious directions

1. Bad Luck—also known as ho hai in Chinese. This brings mild bad luck that is more aggravating than severe. It is usually manifested by obstacles that delay your success, cause you to lose your cool, and are generally very annoying. But it is not serious so the bad luck brought is usually bearable. Nevertheless, these are the kind of things we can all do without!

2. Five Ghosts—also known as wu kwei. This is more serious as it suggests that there are troublesome people in your life who make you miserable, unhappy, and stressed out!

Usually the five ghosts refers to troublemakers in the office, people who politic against you and those who cause you problems by gossiping about you and spreading malicious, untrue or exaggerated stories about you. This kind of bad luck can transform into evil! It is a direction you really must avoid!

3. Six Killings—also known as lui shar. This direction is even worse than the five ghosts as it involves six kinds of misfortune that stab at your heart causing you grief, heartbreak, and terrible sufferings. It usually refers to the loss of a loved one, money or assets, your good name, friendship, home, or the loss of good health. This too is a direction to avoid at all costs.

4. Total Loss—also known as chueh ming. This is the ultimate bad luck direction, which can result in you losing everything that is dear to you, and necessary for your survival— perhaps through a natural disaster like a tsunami, or the financial meltdown of 2008. It is an extremely unlucky direction that should always be avoided.

Your Kua Number	1	2	3	4	5*	6	7	8	9
INAUSPICIOUS DIRECTIONS									
Your ho hai (Bad luck direction)	W	E	SW	NW	E S	SE	N	S	NE
Your wu kwei (five ghosts direction)	NE	SE	NW	SW	SE N	E	S	N	W
Your lui sha (six killings direction)	NW	S	NE	W	S E	N	SE	E	SW
Your chueh ming (total loss direction)	SW	N	W	NE	N SE	S	E	SE	NW

* Kua Number 5, the top numbers are for men, and those below are for women

Using your lucky directions   89

If you make an effort to use this eight-mansions method of eight directions feng shui, based on your Kua Number, you will find that, over time, life becomes a lot easier and more pleasant for you—good and auspicious feng shui is quite magical but when good luck happens it sort of creeps up on you. It does not occur in any dramatic fashion and it will only be as you look back over a month's practice or so that you come to realize that indeed life has become more pleasant, people are being nicer to you, opportunities are indeed opening up, and you are feeling more lucky.

To use your good-luck directions, it is a good idea to commit your four lucky directions to memory and then to always carry a pocket compass so that you never inadvertently end up facing a bad luck direction. We have seen just how bad these negative directions can be, so whenever you are involved in doing something relatively important such as facing a customer, your boss, your client, or simply interacting with friends, then even just shifting your weight to face your good direction will make a difference!

At first you might find this odd, but after a week of practice it will become second nature for you. Obviously you should also arrange all your sitting-room chairs and your bed to benefit every member of the family so that all are sitting and facing their good luck directions whenever possible.

Face your lucky directions according to your Kua Number.

Avoiding your unlucky directions   90

While it is excellent to always face an auspicious direction whenever you are engaged in a productive pursuit, it is even more important to ensure that you never ever have to face your personalized unlucky direction. This is something you should consciously work at avoiding especially now that you have been made aware that there is indeed such a thing as a bad luck bringing direction.

You would not believe how many of my most successful consultations have been simply rearranging furniture at work for people so they sit facing an auspicious direction. Those who had suffered from facing their bad direction almost always saw a difference immediately. These were among my most satisfying moments as it was also easy to help them maintain their much improved feng shui. Teaching people to use this eight-mansions method of feng shui has always led them to wanting to learn more and it is usually only after using this method that they graduate on to learning flying star, another method which, of course, use numbers and directions of the compass.

Always face an auspicious direction when at home.

91 Incorporating the formula into your lifestyle

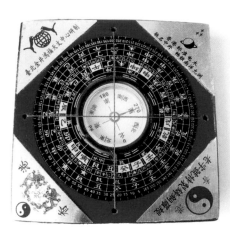

The Lo Shu compass gives the principle feng shui formulas.

Since this is a personalized formula, it is best practiced by incorporating it into your personal lifestyle so that you always use your best directions when working, sleeping, and undertaking any kind of activity. All that is needed is for you to learn your own set of good-luck and bad-luck directions and to carry a small compass around so that you are never caught in a situation where you have to sit facing a total-loss direction.

Eight mansions is so easy to practice because it is exclusively about orientations: all that is required is for you to tap into your auspicious directions. It goes to the heart of feng shui because it uses orientations to ensure that you are always blending into the chi energy of your space.

Find and face your good direction

In instances where sitting or sleeping in the desired direction is not physically possible, you should try to use at least one of your other three good directions. It may not be the direction you want but it is infinitely better to sit facing an acceptable direction than to sit facing one that is inauspicious and spells total loss for you!

The formula describes the specific types of good and bad luck of all the eight directions of the compass but whenever you are unable to tap the direction that you want then it is a good idea to be creative about your feng shui arrangement of furniture. In the practice of feng shui, you will find that on a practical level you always need to decide on the trade offs involved—perhaps giving up something in order to achieve some particular feng shui arrangement. When it comes to sleeping and facing directions at home, however, if there is a choice between getting hit by poison arrows or successfully tapping your direction then it is better to be protected from the poison arrow first!

92 What your Kua Number says about you

Your Kua Number also tells you your personal Kua element, and your personal trigram for feng shui purposes. This is summarized for all the nine numbers in the table here, showing all the information you need about elements and your directions for personal growth. These will help you to "feng shui" your personal space, to custom design color schemes, as well as the shapes and directions that benefit you personally according to your Kua Number.

Kua Number	Your Kua element	Your Kua trigram	Best color for your home	Best direction for personal growth
1	Water	Kan	White	North
2	Earth	Kun	Red/yellow	Southwest
3	Wood	Chen	Blue/green	East
4	Wood	Sun	Blue/green	Southeast
5	Earth	Kun/ken	Red/yellow	SW/NE
6	Metal	Chien	Yellow/white	Northwest
7	Metal	Tui	Yellow/white	West
8	Earth	Ken	Red/yellow	Northeast
9	Fire	Li	Green/red	South

Lucky things for Kua 1 people   93

In eight mansions feng shui, your Kua Number is considered your lucky number for feng shui purposes. With a Kua Number of 1, use it to activate good fortune and success in your living space. Examples of this include selecting the 1st day of each month to undertake important projects, to have numbers end with the number 1, and even have the number printed on your T-shirt or monogrammed onto your sports jacket!

This is particularly suitable for people who live alone and for the feng shui of small office spaces. So if your Kua Number is 1, then you know that Water is your personal element and that having a water feature is sure to benefit you. Likewise locating yourself in the north sector of a room or office is certain to bring benefits. And if you sit facing north it will be very beneficial for you in that this is the direction that brings personal growth, making you happy and energized.

Stay bright and white

The best color for you is white, as this is the color that has the best natural affinity for you. Wearing white will bring you the luck of authority and cause others to view you with greater respect. Those in managerial situations would definitely benefit from wearing white. Metallic colors such as gold and silver are also excellent for you, as are dark blue and black—the colors of water—so wearing both black and white benefits you.

Surrounding yourself with metal windchimes and bells placed in the north corners of your living or work space will strengthen and empower you. People who belong to Kua 1 always benefit from wearing white gold jewelry, especially those set with blue stones such as sapphires and aquamarines.

Kua 1 people benefit from white, airy spaces.

Auspicious factors for Kua 1

Element	Water
Color	White
Direction	North

Unlucky things for Kua 1 people   94

With Number 1 as your Kua Number, however, you must also be aware of the taboos that can bring negative consequences to your space. Thus you must always ensure that the north sector of your home or office is kept especially uncluttered. Here the best color for the walls is to be painted white and the colors to avoid under all circumstances are shades of green, as well as all types of cream and yellow.

Reduce the amount of plants that suggest an excess of Wood element here as they will cause your Kua sector in the north to become exhausted. Instead place more metal objects or metal furniture in the north.

Those with Kua Number 1 should also reduce the amount of green they wear, as the Wood element energy this represents does nothing for you. In fact it could well exhaust your feng shui. Yellow or earth colors are also not good colors for you. You should avoid wearing crystals, and yellow and green stones—so don't wear emeralds, green tourmalines, and citrines as these could well bring mishaps and obstacles into your life.

95 Lucky things for Kua 2 people

Earth tones and pairs of items enhance life for Kua 2 people.

Auspicious factors for Kua 2

Element	Earth
Color	Red/yellow
Direction	Southwest

Knowing all the things that bring you luck is sure to help you to feng shui your personal space more effectively and accurately. One of the best ways of doing this is to use your personal Kua Number as a guide to all that is good and bad for you personally as well as for your space.

If your Kua Number is 2, Earth energy is superb for you, as Big Earth is your personal element, so having some kind of mountain-type feature nearby is sure to benefit you. This can be a painting hanging behind you, or the presence of a globe, perhaps made of crystal or some kind of ceramic material. The presence of the Earth element will instantly strengthen your environmental feng shui, and if you have these enhancers in a pair it is even better because it emphasizes the number 2 that is so lucky for you.

Enhance the southwest

Likewise, locating yourself in the southwest sector of your room, or the southwest corner of the office is certain to bring benefits for you as this is the direction that brings personal growth, making you effective and very productive. It will also attract powerful women into your life who have the inclination to help you! To make the southwest even more powerful place a bright red lamp here.

The best colors for you are the earth tones—from yellow to golden—with red also suitable, Wearing earthy colors if you are also well tanned will make the Earth Goddess of the southwest very auspicious and enhance your personal feng shui. In terms of the gemstones those that suit you best are the golden topazes, the citrines, and all the red stones such as rubies. Crystals are also excellent for you as these activate the Earth energies of the cosmic universe in a very efficient way so wearing crystals, and better yet diamonds, will enhance your personal feng shui enormously.

96 Unlucky things for Kua 2 people

A diamond brings good luck to Kua 2, but gold on its own may be unlucky.

Everything that is made of metal brings exhausting energy to those with Kua Number 2, and if you wear jewelry it is important to have at least one diamond to bring in the crystal energy. Otherwise gold alone might not be so good for you, but when diamonds or other suitable gemstones are added then the jewelry can bring good fortune.

Metallic colors such as gold and silver are bad for your southwest corner, as are dark green and brown, which are the colors of the Wood element. In fact it is important not to place too many green plants in the southwest direction of your home as this will definitely cause problems for you, bringing obstacles that can even block your success. And if you surround yourself with things made of metal, such as windchimes and bells made of brass, and you place these in the southwest corners of your living or work space, these are sure to weaken you. People who belong to Kua Number 2 always run the risk of being weakened by metallic energies when these are placed in the southwest sector of the house; anywhere else is fine.

Lucky things for Kua 3 people   97

Those whose Kua Number is 3 should note that their personalized element energy is Big Wood, so having a really beautiful tree in the east sector of your garden will create superb feng shui for you. In the past it was known that trees could bring amazingly auspicious feng shui but the tree in question always had to sync perfectly with the energy of the resident. One method, according to old feng shui lore, was for anyone with Kua Number 3 to have a beautiful tree in the east. So if you are Kua 3 then plant a majestic tree there; the grander and more healthy this tree grows the better will be your feng shui. It is important that the tree grows strong—ensure that it does not wither and die!

Those with Kua 3 also benefit from having a room in the east sector of the house or the east corner of any building as an office. The east brings you benefits because it has a natural affinity with you and if you sit facing east it is likewise beneficial. This is the direction that brings personal growth, making you effective and productive.

The best colors for you are those associated with wood—greens and browns. Thus green gemstones are excellent, such as emeralds, jade, and green tourmalines. Blue stones are also beneficial and these include blue topaz, aquamarines, and sapphires. Amethysts can also have excellent effect.

Auspicious factors for Kua 3 people

Element	Wood
Color	Blue/green
Direction	East

Trees planted in the east are brilliant energizers for Kua 3 people.

Unlucky things for Kua 3 people   98

Things made of metal are dangerous for those with Kua Number 3. Metal and Fire together spell extreme danger so it is a good idea to avoid having these two elements in the east sector of the house. Bright lights bring very exhausting energy to Kua 3, and if you wear red add black to balance it out. You must never wear white with red or gold, as these combinations are sure to hurt your luck.

As for wearing jewelry it is better to wear black silk cords than gold chains. When you wear gold on its own, the energy created in your personal auric space tends to be killing and very exhausting, so refrain from wearing decorative gold chains.

Metallic colors such as gold and silver are bad for your east corner, as are the dark red colors associated with the Fire element. In fact it is important not to make the lights in the east too bright as this is sure to cause problems for you, bringing obstacles that may block your success. So go easy on the bright lights in the east sector. And if you surround yourself in the east corners of your living or work space with things made of metal, such as windchimes and bells made of brass, these are sure to weaken you. People who belong to Kua Number 3 always run the risk of being weakened by metallic energies especially when these are accompanied with red colors.

99 Lucky things for Kua 4 people

Green gemstones, such as emerald and jade, are lucky for Kua 4 people.

Those whose Kua Number is 4 should take note that their personalized element energy is Small Wood and that their cosmic force is the wind. Kua 4 people benefit from living in the sectors of their home that are breezy and airy. Their directional location is the southeast, where the element is Wood, symbolized by small plants, flowering shrubs and fresh flowers rather than by tall, towering trees—the kind of plants that can bend with the winds such as bamboo and pines. Having bamboo plants in the southeast is thus extremely beneficial for Kua 4 people.

Those with Kua 4 also benefit from having their bedroom in the southeast sector of the house, or office in the southeast corner of any building. The southeast brings benefits because of the natural affinity that Kua 4 people have with this part of the home—and if you sit facing southeast it brings you the luck of wealth and a good name. The wind of the southeast blows auspiciously for you and this is the direction that brings personal growth, attracting success and recognition for you.

Focus on green

The best colors for you as a Kua 4 person are the lighter greens and the deeper blues. Green gemstones are excellent, such as emeralds and jade, though green tourmalines are less suitable for Kua 4 people. Blue stones are also beneficial and these include blue topaz, aquamarines, and sapphires; amethysts are also excellent. Remember that for you the best things have a blue-green overtone, so blue or green amber is amazingly lucky for you—if you can find this rare stone.

You will also benefit from having some kind of water feature in the southeast, as Water here helps Wood to flourish and grow.

Auspicious factors for Kua 4 people

Element	Wood
Color	Blue/green
Direction	Southeast

100 Unlucky things for Kua 4 people

As with Kua 3 people, Kua 4 people are also averse to all things made of metal. Metal and Fire together signify danger, perhaps even more so than for those with Kua 3, so it is an excellent idea to ensure that the southeast sector of your house is not overly lit. Bright lights situated in the southeast corner are sure to bring obstacles that block your success.

Bright lights exhaust the energy of those with Kua Number 4, so it is not a good idea to wear too much red, or have excessive amount of red clothes inside your wardrobe. Red is a color that is both unfriendly and dangerous for you, and definitely will not bring you much luck at all.

With jewelry it is better to wear black silk cords and to avoid wearing gold chains. Gold on its own does all things negative to you as the energy created is too strong, but add diamonds and colored stones and the energy transforms into something auspicious for you Kua 4 people!

Metallic colors such as gold and silver are also bad for your southeast corner, as are the dark red colors of the Fire element. Nor should there be metallic furniture here—its presence would be sure to cause problems for you,

Gems for Kua 4 people

Lucky and unlucky things for Kua 5 people   101

Everything that is made of metal brings exhausting energy to those with Kua Number 5, and this is because the Metal element brings depleting vibes to the Earth chi of number 5 people. This is a powerful Earth element number that has special strength during the current Period of 8 and it is also a number that brings misfortunes to everyone. However, if you are Kua 5, the number 5 in the charts has the potential to bring you transformational luck, the kind that can turn negative energies into positive.

Women with Kua 5 have the same attributes as those with Kua 8, while men with Kua 5 follow those with Kua 2 so you can read the sections on these two Kua Numbers to gain greater insights into your Kua Number depending on your gender.

The strength of Earth

But it definitely a fact that those with Kua 5 are naturally strong Earth people who benefit hugely from the presence of crystals around them, and the older these crystals are the better; they also benefit greatly from wearing lots of colored gemstones and these must be natural and mined from the ground—citrines and amethysts being especially nourishing for Kua 5 people.

What is also good for Kua 5 people is bright fiery red energy—the power of the Fire element strengthens and empowers the chi strength of 5: if you wear red you will attract success easily and effortlessly. A good idea is to place a bright chandelier in the middle of the home to activate the power of the original 5 of the Lo Shu square.

Auspicious factors for Kua 5 people

Element	Earth
Color	Red/yellow
Direction	Men: Southwest
	Women: Northeast

Wearing red and having bright lights and candle flames attracts the energy of Fire, which brings success to Kua 5 people. As Kua 5s are linked also with the Earth element, they benefit greatly from the presence of crystals, such as amethyst (left) and citrine (above).

102 Lucky things for Kua 6 people

A bedroom in the northwest of your home decorated in earth colors brings excellent luck for Kua 6 people.

Everything that is made of metal—gold and silver—brings excellent energy to those with Kua Number 6, and if you wear jewelry, the thicker the gold the better. Kua 6 people are energized by the Metal element so for them gold and fine jewelry does a great deal

Auspicious factors for Kua 6 people

Element	Metal
Color	Yellow/white
Direction	Northwest

indeed. Wearing jewelry is definitely very lucky for you.

You also benefit from wearing white and metallic colors such as gold and silver and your northwest corner should be painted white to maintain the strength of the pure white energy here. Kua 6 people are best located in the northwest corner and this is the sector that also stands for the patriarch and for heavenly energy. Locating your bedroom here is excellent feng shui for you... It is also good to activate the northwest with auspicious symbols of good fortune, all done in brass or metal.

Another good element for the northwest will be the Earth element since this produces the element of the sector. So earthy colors are extremely suitable for the northwest corner.

Surrounding yourself with things made of metal such as windchimes and bells made of brass and placing them in the northwest corners of your living or workspace is sure to strengthen you. People who belong to Kua Number 6 always benefit from metallic energies.

103 Unlucky things for Kua 6 people

Things that suggest Fire element energy are dangerous for those with Kua Number 6 because Fire consumes Metal energy, causing it to dissolve and melt. Fire spells extreme danger so it is a good idea to avoid having excessively bright lighting, a fireplace, or the kitchen in the northwest part of the house. These are harmful from a feng shui perspective and are more so for those whose Kua Number is 6. The northwest is associated with heaven, so having Fire here is like having fire at heaven's gate.

Bright lights bring destructive energy to those with Kua Number 6, and if you wear red it is

important to add black to balance out the red. You must never wear red on its own as this simply brings killing energy towards your persona. Red as a color choice is sure to hurt your luck.

As for wearing jewelry, it is better to wear gold chains than silk cords. When you wear gold on its own, the energy created in your personal auric space is empowering. and when you add diamonds your luck will increase even more.

Gold enhanced with diamonds boosts luck; silk cords deplete it.

Lucky things for Kua 7 people   104

Kua 7 people are also energized by the Metal element so that everything that is made of metal—gold and silver—will enhance your luck bringing excellent energy that attracts strength, success, and prosperity. The number 7 was very strong during the Period of 7 but now that it has been replaced by the Period of 8 it has lost much of its luster and its strength.

As such, what is needed for Kua 7 people is to activate the power of 7. You can do this by hanging a large metallic bell in the west and hitting the bell on a daily basis. This introduces much needed yang chi for the west. If you can, try to make these bells give off a lingering sound—the kind that monks in Tibet and Nepal use to strengthen their meditations. Even if your bell cannot give off a tuneful sound placing it in the west is still extremely beneficial.

Use gold to boost success

Those of you who like wearing jewelry to enhance your personal feng shui are sure to be pleased to hear that this is indeed the best recommendation for Kua 7 people. The more gold you wear the better will be your success luck. Kua 7 people are energized by the Metal element so for them gold and fine jewelry does a great deal indeed.

You also benefit from wearing white and metallic colors such as gold and silver and your west corner should be painted white to activate its own Metal element. In the west, crystals are also excellent and this is because Earth is the element of the sector, making earthy colors extremely suitable for you and the sector.

Auspicious factors for Kua 7 people

Element	Metal
Color	Yellow/white
Direction	West

Placing a metallic bell in the west helps Kua 7s.

Unlucky things for Kua 7 people   105

Those of you who belong to Kua 7 must avoid being too closely allied to both the Fire and Water elements. They can both weaken you, sap you of your strength and energy, and cause your good fortune luck to leak out, so do be careful with the lighting of your home. You must also not place water in the west as this is sure to hurt you.

Things that suggest Fire element energy are dangerous for those with Kua Number 7 and this is because Fire consumes Metal energy, causing it to dissolve and melt. Avoid having bright lights or a fireplace in the west. Another thing to avoid here is the placement of water as the Water element depletes the energy of Metal. Avoid the colors blue and black here as carefully as you avoid red.

When wearing gemstones it is vital that you never wear dark blue stones such as sapphires or lapis—these will cause you to lose your luck. In fact, any kind of blue stone is to be seriously avoided. As for clothes, Kua 7 people should avoid wearing too much black—black is one of the most harmful colors for those who belong to Kua 7.

Water in the west

Check out the placement of Fire, such as a fireplace, and Water in your home, in terms of water features, sinks, and bathrooms.

106 Lucky things for Kua 8 people

As we are currently in the Period of 8 those whose Kua Number is 8 are sure to enjoy some exceptional luck. All the way through to February 4 2024, Kua 8 people will benefit from the contemporary strength of 8 and as we move deeper into the period, those with this Kua Number will feel its benevolent energy even more.

Knowing all the things that bring you luck can help you double your luck and, in fact, it is worthwhile to go to a great deal of trouble to activate and energize your northeast location with Earth element energy—the kind that is sure to attract good fortune vibes for you. It would benefit you enormously to make the northeast your personal space, so try to activate it by making certain it is well-lit as Fire energy will strengthen your Earth chi.

Another must-have for the northeast is a picture or painting of a big mountain range. Supplement this with a large crystal geode—this will bring in the power of the great Earth energy—or place a globe image or solid crystal or glass balls here.

Auspicious factors for Kua 8 people

Element	Earth
Color	Red/yellow
Direction	Northeast

Meanwhile the best color for Kua 8 people are the earth tones—from yellow to golden although red is also very suitable. Earth tones have the best natural affinity for you.

Utilize the Period of 8

Remember that the northeast is the sector of the current Period of 8. It is a west-group direction and location and it is also an axis direction so is extremely powerful. The best thing you can do if your Kua Number is 8 is to stay here and then energize the power of 8 with a crystal 8 containing specks of gold.

107 Unlucky things for Kua 8 people

Everything that is made of metal brings exhausting energy to those with Kua Number 8, and if you wear jewelry it is important to have at least one diamond so that its powerful energy will let the Earth chi stay in control.

The color white, as well as all kinds of metallic colors, are bad for your northeast corner, as are dark green and brown, which are the colors of the Wood element. In fact, it is important not to place too many green plants in the northeast location of your home as this will cause problems for you, bringing obstacles that block your success. So go easy on the plants in the northeast sector and if you would naturally like to surround yourself in your living or work space with things made of metal such as windchimes and bells, resist the urge as these will sap you of your strength. People who belong to Kua Number 8 always run the risk of being weakened by metallic energies when these are placed in the northeast sector of the house. Anywhere else is fine.

Diamonds protect Kua 8 people against the exhausting influence of metal.

Lucky things for Kua 9 people 108

When your Kua Number is 9, it can bring you the power of the element of Fire. The number 9 also signifies future prosperity, so those of you who belong to Kua 9 should immediately take note of your auspicious east-group directions and simultaneously create an oasis of red, fiery energy located in the south sector of your home. In this way, you will be activating the number 9 and tapping into its current strong energy at the same time.

So, what is good for Kua 9 people? Basically, anything that suggests the Fire element, so things that are bright, to do with sunshine, and the color red. The element of Wood is also excellent so everything that grows—which means healthy, growing plants—can symbolically and cosmically feed and strengthen Fire element energy.

Auspicious factors for Kua 9 people

Element	Fire
Color	Green/red
Direction	South

Emphasize red

In the south, which is the direction of the number, have red curtains or carpets, or paint the walls here bright red! Also display lots of healthy plants and blooming flowers.

The south is the place of the horse and the phoenix—both will bring excellent recognition luck. For speedy success, place a symbolic nine-horses ornament here, and for opportunities that increase your net worth, place nine phoenixes in the south.

Red brings success for Kua 9 people, so have lots of it in the south of your home to energize your luck.

Unlucky things for Kua 9 people 109

What may not be so helpful in the south is the presence of Water. Fire and Water elements clash directly, so it is best not to have excessive amounts of water here. A water feature such as a pond, a pool, or an aquarium can have the effect of putting Fire out, so it is usually best to keep water well away from the south of a property.

Another element that could hurt and exhaust Fire energy is the element of Earth, so crystals and other Earth element objects should not be placed in the south. Earth exhausts Fire and this presence in excess in the south will create blockages to your energy here.

Wood energy is fine in the south, as it supports Fire in the five-element cycle.

110 Updating your lucky/unlucky directions each year

Because the luck of your home changes each year, it's important to update its feng shui, which may mean moving furniture around so that you sit, eat, and sleep in more fortuitous directions.

While your Kua Number points to your lucky directions that bring the four kinds of good fortune, it is necessary to update the chi energy that directly affects each of the eight directions. This is one of the most fundamental aspects of feng shui practice that has been largely ignored by many practitioners, as a result of which there could be years when the direction that signifies your Kua Number could well be afflicted by the chi energy of the year. If you then face that direction or place yourself in that location during the year you could succumb to one of the afflictions.

You should note that directions can get hurt by a variety of factors that change every year, and it is for this reason that the Chinese master practitioners of feng shui always refer to the annual almanac to check the flying star charts as well as the stars of the 24 mountains that are in play for any given year. Learning the methods of investigation requires knowledge of the Chinese esoteric systems that underpin the Chinese lunar and solar calendars; but choosing instead not to update the directions each year could sometimes prove fatal.

How to find your annual updates

To assist those wanting to update their directions each year, we have two sources that anyone interested may refer to every year. All the annual updates are available free at my website. Look for the year's page, so for 2011 go to www.wofs.com/2011. You can also get the annual astrological Fortune 7 Feng Shui books, which contain the full analysis by animal sign in great and comprehensive detail. These books can be obtained online at www.fsmegamall.com or at www.wofs.com.

Update every year

Updating your Kua direction each year suggests that wherever remedies are needed you will know what to put in that direction; sometimes you may also be told not to face that direction in that year in order to avoid the affliction lying there. Practiced in this way, your use of feng shui becomes a dynamic and interactive activity; it also becomes a great deal more effective.

Using Kua Numbers when choosing homes   111

Once you are in possession of your Kua Number, you will know your four auspicious directions; one way to use this information is to select the most ideal home that you will be able to synchronize with your own inner feng shui chi energy.

Feng shui experts all agree that the best feng shui house for anyone is the house that faces the direction of their Kua Number's sheng chi direction. Thus, if your Kua Number is 1, then your sheng chi direction is southeast. If you can find a house with a southeast facing direction it will be excellent for you. Generally speaking, it is ideal to follow the sheng chi direction of the patriarch of the household. It is assumed that what benefits him will definitely benefit everyone else, irrespective of their own Kua Number.

If you find a house whose facing direction is in sync with your Kua Number you must then check how you would live in the house according to the four sectors of good fortune and the four sectors of misfortune. The eight mansions formula can be used as the basis for arranging the layout and the allocation of the rooms for residents.

The eight charts are reproduced on the next page, and these can be used as a guide for selecting a home according to your Kua Number.

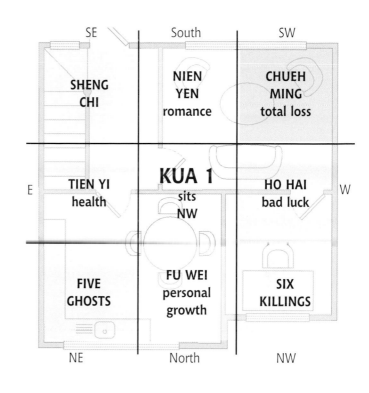

SE	South	SW
SHENG CHI	**NIEN YEN** romance	**CHUEH MING** total loss
E **TIEN YI** health	**KUA 1** sits NW	**HO HAI** bad luck W
FIVE GHOSTS	**FU WEI** personal growth	**SIX KILLINGS**
NE	North	NW

Living in a house that faces your sheng chi direction brings success. This house has the door in the southeast so faces southeast, making it perfect for Kua 1 people.

112 Using Kua Numbers to select rooms

When allocating rooms, place east-group people in eastern-facing rooms, with west-group people in western-facing rooms.

You can also use your Kua Number and your auspicious directions to choose the rooms in the house that will bring you good fortune. Indeed allocating the rooms of the home or office according to the Kua Numbers of those who will occupy them is one of the most effective way of ensuring that the energy of the home or office is harmoniously allocated.

This is one of the best ways to use the Kua Number, mainly because it reveals your good and bad luck directions. The main rule is to place all east group people into east direction rooms and west-group people into the west direction rooms. You must use a compass to determine these directional locations and it is best done on site. Later you can use a floor plan to start designing the layout and the allocation of rooms.

Pay particular attention to the room you choose to be the master bedroom, because in the feng shui of any space the Patriarch and the Matriarch should enjoy the best feng shui sectors of the home. This is because their luck always has the strongest impact on the overall luck for the residents. When the luck of these two key residents is good then everyone else will enjoy the reflected glory of their good fortune.

Good directions

Sheng chi

Tien yi

Nien yen

Fu wei

Unlucky directions

Ho hai

Five ghosts

Six killings

Chueh ming

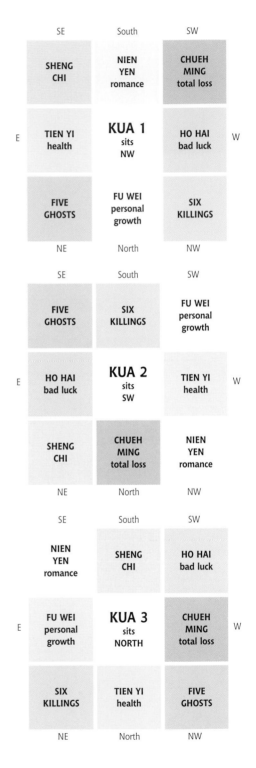

SE	South	SW
SHENG CHI	NIEN YEN romance	CHUEH MING total loss
TIEN YI health (E)	KUA 1 sits NW	HO HAI bad luck (W)
FIVE GHOSTS	FU WEI personal growth	SIX KILLINGS
NE	North	NW

SE	South	SW
FIVE GHOSTS	SIX KILLINGS	FU WEI personal growth
HO HAI bad luck (E)	KUA 2 sits SW	TIEN YI health (W)
SHENG CHI	CHUEH MING total loss	NIEN YEN romance
NE	North	NW

SE	South	SW
NIEN YEN romance	SHENG CHI	HO HAI bad luck
FU WEI personal growth (E)	KUA 3 sits NORTH	CHUEH MING total loss (W)
SIX KILLINGS	TIEN YI health	FIVE GHOSTS
NE	North	NW

SE	South	SW
FU WEI personal growth	TIEN YI health	FIVE GHOSTS
NIEN YEN romance	**KUA 4** sits NW	SIX KILLINGS
CHUEH MING total loss	SHENG CHI	HO HAI bad luck
NE	North	NW

(E on left, W on right)

SE	South	SW
SIX KILLINGS	FIVE GHOSTS	TIEN YI health
CHUEH MING total loss	**KUA 7** sits SE	FIVE GHOSTS
NIEN YEN romance	HO HAI bad luck	SHENG CHI
NE	North	NW

(E on left, W on right)

SE	South	SW
CHUEH MING total loss	HO HAI bad luck	SHENG CHI
SIX KILLINGS	**KUA 5/8** sits NE	NIEN YEN romance
FU WEI personal growth	FIVE GHOSTS	TIEN YI health
NE	North	NW

(E on left, W on right)

SE	South	SW
TIEN YI health	FU WEI personal growth	SIX KILLINGS
SHENG CHI	**KUA 9** sits WEST	FIVE GHOSTS
HO HAI bad luck	NIEN YEN romance	CHUEH MING total loss
NE	North	NW

(E on left, W on right)

SE	South	SW
HO HAI bad luck	CHUEH MING total loss	NIEN YEN romance
FIVE GHOSTS	**KUA 6** sits EAST	SHENG CHI
TIEN YI health	SIX KILLINGS	FU WEI personal growth
NE	North	NW

(E on left, W on right)

Remember that the direction in which the house sits is directly opposite its facing direction. Note the four good directions (sheng chi, health, romance, and personal growth) and the four unlucky directions (ho hai, five ghosts, six killings, and total loss). Identify your lucky and unlucky rooms accordingly.

The Tao of numbers— trinities and quarters

While your Birth Number is central to the Taoist philosophy it also places great emphasis on pairs and groups of numbers—most strikingly evoked by the trinity of tien ti ren, heaven, earth and man. Find the significance of pairs, the four cardinal directions, the eight compass points, and the 24 mountains of luck as well as the significance of three-, four-, and eight-sided shapes.

Your day of birth is your Taoist lucky number 113

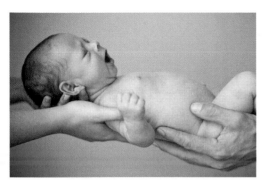

A great many feng shui beliefs, especially those related to the role of numbers in luck enhancement, come from the Tao, which looks on life's existence as a journey to wholeness; an esoteric blend on the philosophy of living against a background of transformative chi energy.

Taoist philosophy has many layers of meaning but in a feng shui context, the Tao looks on the origin of the cosmos as a relationship between the mother and the child. The key to a secure and auspicious life is when the child is able to hold on fast to the mother, and here the term mother signifies the formless aspect of the Tao. The "child," meanwhile, refers to a multitude of shifting forms.

So the day you are born is the day the mother gives birth to the child and that day is regarded as a lucky day for the child. As such from a Taoist viewpoint the day of one's birth—the number that you remember as being your birthday—becomes in effect your lucky number. If you follow the Chinese calendar then you should use the Chinese day of birth but if you generally use the Western calendar system you should use that to determine your lucky Taoist number.

The luckiest number of all

Taoists believe that the key number that goes into your subconscious eventually becomes the luckiest number for you and one's birthday possesses this vital attribute. For instance, if you were born on January 9 then the number 9 will automatically become your lucky Taoist number. Everything with 9 in it will then attract good fortune—your house address, your car number, your telephone numbers, or the days you choose to do important activities such as signing a contract or starting a new project.

Here there is no need to reduce your lucky Taoist number to a single digit, although of course you may do so if you feel so inclined. The Tao allows for individual preferences because it is the individual collective unconscious that assigns powerful luck energy strengths to the number in question.

But it is as easy to simply stay with the number of birth so if you are born on the 24th of the month then the number 24 becomes your lucky number. Many people have used this concept of the lucky Taoist number to bet on the roulette wheel, to play with numbers, and for all sorts of speculative activity with great success. They view this as their ultimate lucky number, more so than under any other method of calculation it would seem. So you might want to test this out.

I was born on January 11 so I consider the number 11 to be extremely lucky for me—and it has been. For thirty years the number 11 has always brought some truly yummy goodies into my life—and needless to say my home address is also number 11, so I have systematically tapped into this lucky number of mine.

The day of your birth can become one of your lucky numbers—having your birth number as your house numbers, or lucky numbers for competitions, maximizes your luck potential.

114 The trinity of tien ti ren—heaven, earth, and man

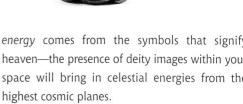

In Taoism, the concept of the trinity is also an important aspect of life's changing fortunes, in particular the concept of tien ti ren—or heaven, earth, and humankind: the trinity of luck. It is believed that not only does this concept point out that we are all ruled by three different kinds of luck—what we are born with, what we surround ourselves with (our feng shui), and what we do with our life (our actions), but the Taoists go further and point out that luck is a three-pointed trinity, that there must be the triangle of forces from heaven, earth, and form within ourselves for luck to flow freely into our lives.

For there to be good fortune, there must be all three kinds of chi energy present whether in the home, the office, or the business premises. *Heaven*

energy comes from the symbols that signify heaven—the presence of deity images within your space will bring in celestial energies from the highest cosmic planes.

Orientate yourself and your home

Earth energy comes from good orientations and the successful arranging of space according to feng shui principles, while *Humankind energy* comes from your own vitality, your own vibrancy and internal energy levels. So collective good fortune is usually more than just feng shui, it is in fact a good marriage of these three types of energies.

What we must do is ensure the presence of good heaven energy; either it needs to be activated through the chanting of prayers or reciting of mantras, or it must be created by arranging regular food and other offerings in formal prayer sessions. In other words, for anyone to really enjoy good fortune this premier trinity of forces has to be present.

Displaying deity images, such as Chinese gods, brings in heaven luck. Good feng shui and good orientations for your home creates earth and humankind luck.

Four friends of the astrology zodiac 115

More than the trinity is the foursome in Taoist good-fortune reckonings. Thus Chinese astrological systems always stress the groups of four that make up the special foursome in the astrological good-fortune stakes. This refers to animal signs that are particularly good for one another, so that knowing which of the three sets of four animal groupings you belong to enables you not only to differentiate between those who are your friends and those who may not be, but also enables you to activate your space with auspicious images from the animal zodiac that are beneficial for you. Check the chart opposite to discover your special astrological allies, and your "secret friend"—the one whose help and assistance may not be so obvious to you.

Your allies and secret friend

To become knowledgeable about your friends and allies just see the groupings here and commit them to memory.

Animal sign	Three zodiac allies	One secret friend
Rat	rat plus dragon & monkey	ox
Ox	ox plus snake & rooster	rat
Tiger	tiger plus horse & dog	boar
Rabbit	rabbit plus sheep & boar	dog
Dragon	dragon plus rat & monkey	rooster
Snake	snake plus rooster & ox	monkey
Horse	horse plus tiger & dog	sheep
Sheep	sheep plus rabbit & boar	horse
Monkey	monkey plus dragon & rat	snake
Rooster	rooster plus snake & ox	dragon
Dog	dog plus horse & tiger	rabbit
Boar	boar plus sheep & rabbit	tiger

Helpful and unhelpful people

The Chinese are always so sensitive about whether people are "helpful" or "unhelpful" in an astrological context, even having special names to describe them. So, for instance, those unhelpful or harmful are often described as the "devil people in your life." Good luck always refers to mentors coming into your life to help you, while one of the worst kinds of misfortune luck is often described as meeting up with "devil people," or those who would cause you harm and therefore should always be avoided.

Each animal has two allies in Chinese astrology. The dog's allies are the horse and the tiger. His secret friend is the rabbit. Looking up your allies helps identify your true friends in life.

Secret friend

116 Three seasonal animals of astrology

Wintertime is auspicious for the rat, boar, and ox.

In addition to the zodiac alliances shown in Tip 115, there is another trinity of astrological signs that also point to auspicious energy being created through the chi changes that transform luck from season to season. It is thus useful to note that there are four groupings to signify the four seasons, with each group comprising three animal signs, as shown on the chart below. When they are present within the same family they generate a great deal of special luck energy during the season they represent. The best combination consists of the mother, the father, and one child.

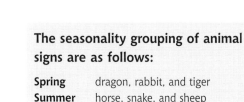

The seasonality grouping of animal signs are as follows:

Spring	dragon, rabbit, and tiger
Summer	horse, snake, and sheep
Fall	rooster, dog, and monkey
Winter	rat, boar, and ox

117 The significance of the three peaks

The number 3 is always significant in the feng shui aspects of events and developments, so good things, therefore, are believed to always happen in groups of three. Thus magical incantations and prayers are usually recited three times and feng shui rituals always insist that these are done three times.

As such, one of the most auspicious symbols of good fortune is the sign of the three peaks or three mountains. According to feng shui lore, having three mountain peaks within sight of your front door is a sign that the sons of the family will rise to great prominence as leaders, and bring great honor and wealth to the family.

If you do not have this kind of auspicious view, then you can artificially create it by placing a symbolic "three peaks" on top of your front wall. Here the operative number is three, which creates a special numerical energy that enables the next generation's good fortune to be felt and enjoyed by the current generation.

A painting or photograph of three mountains symbolizes success for sons.

A pair of birds brings opportunities 118

In addition to the trinity the Tao is also very big on pairs, and, in fact, in feng shui good fortune is said always to come in pairs, so when you want to attract opportunities and good news into the home a pair of winged creatures is always very effective. In this context the presence of a pair of phoenix, for instance, flanking the front door, is successful for attracting lucky opportunities for all the residents within.

Look for animal pairs and display them in your home for good luck.

A pair of celestials brings protection 119

For protection it is beneficial to turn to the celestial creatures that serve as local protectors. In feng shui there are several kinds to choose from, the most popular of which are fu dogs, chi lins, and pi yaos—all of which are traditional protectors that are widely used and displayed in many Chinese cities, guarding not just homes but also public places including museums, libraries, government offices, temples, palaces, and, these days, even restaurants and shopping malls.

To be effective, however, these celestials are always placed in pairs—male and female, yin and yang—and always flanking the door. The number two is even, yin in nature, and thus very auspicious not just at the material level but also along parallel planes of existence making it the ideal number to be invoked as a guardian.

For protection, therefore, it is an excellent idea to have these guardians protect all the entrances of your home.

Two matching animal statues act as symbolic door guardians to protect your home.

120 The concept of "double goodness"

To take the idea of doubling further, it is also beneficial to note here the Taoist concept of "double goodness:" that everything good, everything protective, and everything auspicious is always more effective when invoked as a pair. Thus Taoist masters always recommend that anything auspicious placed in your house should be in pairs to attract luck, whether it is a pair of wealth vases; a pair of elephants, a pair of crystal balls, or simply a paired item of furniture.

Even numbers can be activated in pairs. So if 8 is your good luck number then having a double 8—as in 88—will double the good luck. This then is the concept of the double goodness. In this current period of, course, there is nothing luckier than the double 8.

When displaying objets d'art, pairs are always more fortuitous than single items. Lamps in pairs strengthen the symbolism.

121 The four seasons of good fortune

Having an image of the four seasons in your home brings good fortune.

To ensure that you enjoy good luck all year round it is also necessary to think of creating good fortune through all the four seasons. Thus if you are observant enough you will find that in many old Chinese—homes where landscape masterpieces are extremely popular—there will always be paintings of the same scene done over four seasons. In each of these paintings all the most auspicious symbols associated with each season—the flowers, trees, fruits, insects, and objects associated with Summer, Spring, Fall, and Winter—will all be present. This is to ensure that the home where the paintings hang will enjoy continued honor, abundance, and prosperity through the whole year.

The four-season painting is in fact the principal feng shui energizer that was extremely popular during the old days.

The four cardinal directions 122

The number 4 is also very prominently associated with the four cardinal directions—north, south, east and west. These four directions are represented by the rat, the rabbit, the horse and the rooster. In Chinese feng shui, however, these four directions are so powerful that houses are deliberately oriented just a little bit off the four cardinal directions—throughout history only temples and palaces have been felt to be suitable to face exactly north, south, east or west.

However, the four cardinal directions are vital sectors of any home and they should be carefully energized by placing either the astrological animal signs or, better yet, the relevant one of the four celestial guardians.

In addition to the four celestial creatures there are also the all-powerful Four Heavenly Kings—these are Buddhist deities that over the centuries have found their way into feng shui legend mainly because they are such fearsome and effective protectors. The Four Heavenly Kings protect households against falling victim to physical disaster—floods, fires, hurricanes, earthquakes, viruses, epidemics, and all other calamities, both natural and manmade. These attributes make them extremely relevant these days when the world seems to be rocked with so many natural disasters brought by wind, rain, and fire... As such there has been a big revival in their popularity as the four most powerful of home guardians.

Find the right guardian for each sector

Placing a set of celestials activates the guardianship of these exceptional feng shui creatures—their chi energy is what brings good fortune to the home. Use the following celestial creature in each sector:

East	dragon
South	phoenix
North	tortoise
West	tiger

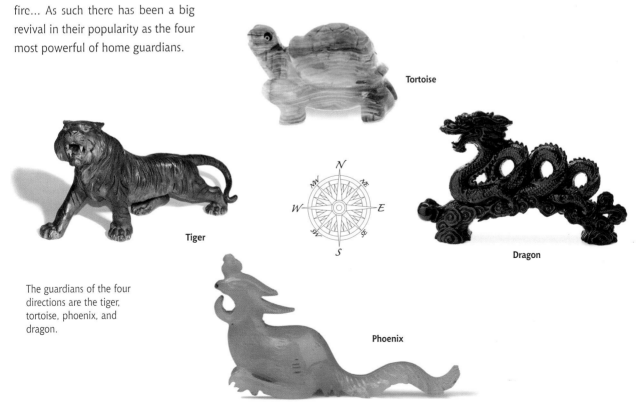

Tortoise

Tiger

Dragon

Phoenix

The guardians of the four directions are the tiger, tortoise, phoenix, and dragon.

123 The eight compass directions

In feng shui, the number 8 figures again and again as a very lucky number and it is probably the most visible of all of them. The most relevant associations linked to this number are the eight compass directions that feature prominently in many feng shui methods and formulas. Each of the eight directions occupies 45 degrees of the compass space and these radiate outwards from a center point. The demarcation into eight directions suggest that it is these eight sides or directional points that are the best "anchors" for the persona of individuals hence making eight a very significant number.

Compass directions by themselves are actually meaningless and they have no relevance on their own. They only become useful when there is a

The compass has eight cardinal directions, which links with the good fortune of the 8 of the feng shui Period of 8.

point of reference. So the directions and the orientations associated with them have this inherent quality of emptiness, being without space—in effect they do not occupy any space unless and until the space itself gets designated. Sometimes, in an attempt to be complete, instead of eight directions people talk about ten directions by bringing two additional points of reference—top and bottom—into play. In this context, then, the number 10 also becomes significant.

The Period of 8

Another aspect of the number 8 is that it is also the number of the current feng shui period. We are described as living through the Period of 8 which means that this number is not only lucky and meaningful, it is also very vibrant and strong. Anyone activating the power of eight by displaying its image or ensuring its presence in their lives will find that its energy works fast. In fact, just wearing the number 8 on your body is sufficient to activate the energy of eight and all the goodies associated with its eight directions.

Wearing the number 8 is a way to activate the good-luck energy of the feng shui Period of 8 and the eight compass directions.

The 24 mountains of luck 124

It is also possible to expand the power of 8 into 24, which happens when the 8 is multiplied by the number 3. When each of the eight compass sectors are further divided into three sub-directions, this creates what are known as the 24 mountains in feng shui.

The 24 mountains thus refer to 24 individual directional sectors that each occupy 15 degrees of the compass. Each year, each of these sectors is visited by a "star" which, depending on whether this star is good or bad, determines the kind of luck brought to each of the 24 mountains.

In terms of annual luck, therefore, the Chinese always refers to the almanac to see what kind of star flies into each 15-degree sector; this then forms the basis of annual recommendations on how to enhance good stars and subdue bad stars.

The 24 mountain stars also feature prominently in many of the advanced compass formulas of feng shui; these represent the fine tuning of compass feng shui. In terms of luck, the number 24 is said to be the numerical representation of the mystical knot, which itself is a reflection of the number 8 repeated three times. If you believe in the luck of the mystical knot, then simply wearing it activates the fullness of the 24 mountain energies. This is said to be auspicious.

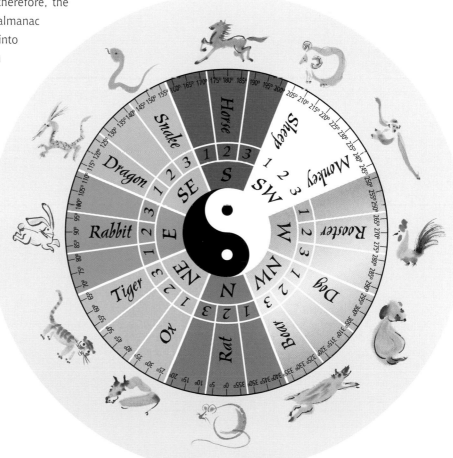

Each of the eight directions divides into three further sectors, or "mountains," of 15 degrees each. Every year a mountain is visited by luck that flies into its sector.

125 Four doorways into the sacred mountain

The Chinese have always believed that there are four doorways through which it is possible to enter the sacred mountain mandala. Here the number 4 reflects again the significance of the quartiles in Chinese numerology, thus there are:

* Four cardinal directions: north, south, east, and west
* Four celestial guardians: the tortoise, tiger dragon, and phoenix
* Four heavenly kings, who guard the four directions
* Four seasons: Spring, Summer, Fall, and Winter
* Finally, there are the four doorways of the mountain mandala, with each showing a different route to the top of the mountain.

The four pathways to success

This suggests that there are always four pathways to success, and activating the sacred mandala means that you will always have options in your life. Should one door close, another will magically open for you. Activating the four pathways, or the four doors, is an excellent way of tapping into this kind of good feng shui—as the symbolism of the four doors says that there is always a way forward in whatever you do.

Activating the magical four

You can activate the magical four by displaying a two- or three-dimensional mandala in your home. You can also hang a picture of a mandala that has a traditional Tibetan-style square as its central image, showing all the four doorways.

Tibetan monks with a mandala made of colored sand—an auspicous three-dimensional mandala.

Four lucky flowers—lotus, peony, chrysanthemum, and magnolia

126

The number four is also extended to the four celestial blooms that attract the luck of good relationships in your life. Thus if you can somehow ensure that the four flowers—the lotus, the peony, the chrysanthemum, and the magnolia—are present in your home, they will immediately suffuse your home with the blooming energy of the four season flowers.

You can show them in pictures, display fake flowers or, best of all, show the real thing. When they bloom in your home it means that your luck has arrived. The symbolism of blooming always means a manifestation of good luck.

The special qualities of the lucky flowers

The peony stands for love and romance and a satisfying sex life. When present, couples enjoy the kind of passion that ignites great love. The peony is a wonderful symbol of romance of the best kind.

The chrysanthemum is the flower of wealth, especially when it comes in yellow. During the lunar new year Chinese families always adorn their homes with this prosperity flower.

The lotus stands for purity and love; this will blossom for you if the lotus starts to flower in your own backyard. This flower also brings perfection.

The orchid brings career success.

127 The special meaning of the circle

There is a connection between numbers and shapes, and in feng shui the interlocking connections and attributes between these two concepts is what gives rise to the connectivity of chi energy. Much of effective feng shui is being able to connect these attributes within a living space in order to create a flow of harmonious chi energy.

Thus the circle, for instance, is usually regarded as the ultimate shape in feng shui. Not only is the circle the shape of heaven but it is also the manifestation of all the numbers that end in zero—meaning 10, 100, 1,000 and so forth. If you wish to become richer, adding increasing number of zeros to your asset wealth, it makes sense to display circles and round shapes in your living space! The circle also stands for the Metal element, which can subdue illness vibes and other misfortune stars.

The never-ending circle

The circle is also associated with never-ending connectivity—with neither a beginning nor an end. For this reason the Chinese always prefer round dining tables, and all the gods of the Chinese pantheon carry double circles when they manifest as protective deities.

The double circle is said to be the tool used to subdue the tiger, while the triple circle is used as a remedy to overcome the annual illness star. Wearing jewelry designed in circles of gold or as concentric circles of diamonds are likewise considered to be very auspicious.

A table symbolizes the circle, the shape of heaven in feng shui.

128 The shape of 3—the triangle

Unlike the smooth circle, the shape of the triangle suggests rising energy—growth as exemplified by Wood feeding the Fire, the element with which it is associated. It is the shape of three and it signifies the holy trinity that brings the power of heaven, earth, and humankind into a collective, auspicious whole.

The triangle is most suited when you have a specific project that requires the patronage of others; when you need to win in a competitive situation or when the odds seem to be against you, then invoking the power of 3 by using the triangle adds greater potency to your space—especially if 3 is also your lucky Birth or Name Number.

Place the triangle in the south as an aide to success and have it in the east to borrow the luck of the Wood element. Triangles are always more powerful when fashioned in red and when the triangle is doubled up we see the powerful six-pointed star. This symbol is, however, connected to the spiritual dimension and is rarely used for advancing success potential.

A simple triangle can be made from a small pillar of stones.

The shape of 4—squares and rectangles   129

The rectangle, in the form of this table, links with the energy of the number 4.

The shapes that make up the figure four are squares and rectangles. The square is the shape of Earth while the rectangle is the shape of Wood. Whether you choose to activate with the square or the rectangle depends not just on whether your lucky Birth or Name Number is 4, but also on what your Kua Number is. Those with Kua Numbers 2, 5, or 8 will benefit from the square shape because this signifies strengthening of the Earth element around them.

Those with Kua Numbers 3 or 4 will benefit from the growth chi of the rectangle. To use shapes around your space think in terms of the tables and desks that you use. Remember that knowing about these attributes of numbers and shapes enables anyone to implement the nuances of many fine points in fong shui that add quite substantially to the harmonious energy of the space around you. The effect may be felt slowly but over time you will begin to notice the difference in your life as increasingly more things go right than wrong.

The shape of 8—the Pa Kua   130

And, finally, the shape of the eight corresponds to the shape of the ultimate feng shui symbol, the Pa Kua—which literally translates to mean "eight sides." The ancients believed that this shape had magical powers associated with the trigrams that are placed around this symbol of feng shui. There are many other esoteric associations connected to the Pa Kua, which is also used as a tool to ward off evil spirits and bad energy.

But the Pa Kua is a powerful symbol and when used in this context it tends also to harm everyone else that stands in its line of fire; it is for this reason that modern practitioners of feng shui prefer not to use the Pa Kua as a protective tool, instead using it as a symbol of the eight aspirations of mankind's luck instead. So, when placing the Pa Kua flat in the home—either as a decorative piece or as a table shape—it epitomizes wealth, health, romance, the luck of descendants, patronage luck, wisdom luck, career luck, and the luck of having a good family name. The eight aspirations it symbolizes in effect incorporate all the different kinds of good fortune that feng shui is able to attract into your life, so energizing the Pa Kua symbol, especially if your lucky number is 8, can be very effective.

The only taboo it is important to remember is to never display the Pa Kua upright facing you in the house, because its rebuttal power is too strong and you could well become sick if you are symbolically hit by its power.

The powerful Pa Kau has eight sides.

Part Seven

Numbers of the Lo Shu and Ho Tu square

The nine numbers that make up the Lo Shu magic square are the basis for the advanced compass formula feng shui. By representing the cycle of the moon, the numbers form a repeating pattern that can be used to find the lucky number for a particular month or year. The Ho Tu combinations are the powerful pairs of numbers found in the square that give added power to the parts of the home they energize.

The magic of the Lo Shu numbers 131

According to Chinese legend, the Lo Shu numbers were originally thought to have been brought to earth on the back of a turtle.

There are 9 numbers in a Lo Shu magic square, the amazing symbol used as a source tool for advanced compass formula feng shui. The Lo Shu square is a three sector by three sector grid comprising nine squares, each occupied by a number from 1 to 9. The original basic Lo Shu square has the number 5 in the center, so that in feng shui, this number is regarded as extremely powerful. The number 5 is an Earth element number, which in the current period has the potential to bring extreme misfortune luck; but for those of you whose Kua Number under the eight mansions formula is 5, then this number instead brings you incredible good luck.

The power of the square

For thousands of years now the Lo Shu square has featured strongly in time dimension feng shui and it represents the numerical aspect of days that track the movement of the waxing and waning moon. The square is regarded almost reverently by practitioners of feng shui and although the original square has 5 in the center, it will change energy pattern and attributes as the numbers "move" or "fly" from grid to grid around the square. This dynamic nature of the Lo Shu square is what gives

The Lo Shu square

Feng shui charts are created using numbers 1 to 9 as shown here —the Lo Shu square. But the Lo Shu flight of stars (see Tip 133) also reveals the Sigil of Saturn and this is believed to be extremely powerful.

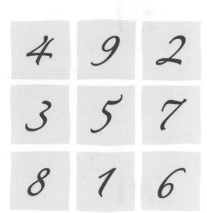

it character and significance, as well as the way the numbers are laid out in the grid.

It is the arrangement of the numbers around the Lo Shu square, however, that is most significant and also most revealing—it is this arrangement of numbers that determines the individual numbers that go into the nine sectors of any house grid, the numbers always following a set pattern. The arrangement also gives rise to the sigils of the square, the esoteric quality that makes the square stand out as a key to unlocking the meanings of other symbols.

132 The Lo Shu square and the significance of number 15

The Chinese prefer to set important dates in the first fifteen days of a calendar month.

The center number of the original square is 5. I use the word "original" because Lo Shu squares of different types can now have any number at the center and this is at the heart of the method that uses this square as a tool of analysis. In the original square, however, 5 is in the center and with this 5 is revealed the significance of the number 15.

Note that the arrangement of numbers in the square shown below shows that every set of three numbers in a straight line—whether horizontally, vertically, or diagonally—adds up to 15. That the sum of any three numbers in a straight line in the

Lo Shu square is 15 is extremely significant, because 15 is the number of days it takes a new moon to wax into a full moon, and for a full moon to wane completely into no moon.

The cycle of the waxing and waning moon is of course the basis of the Chinese lunar calendar, so the significance of the number 15 lies in the way it is the basis for Chinese date keeping. It is for this reason that the Lo Shu square features so strongly in time dimension feng shui. In the selection of auspicious days, the Chinese always prefer to carry out important events—such as opening a new business venture, celebrating an important event, signing a contract, or anything that might have far-reaching consequences—during the first fifteen days of a lunar month when the energy of the moon is waxing, becoming ever brighter and stronger.

This is the significance of the number 15,

4	9	2	→ 4 + 9 + 2 = 15
3	5	7	→ 3 + 5 + 7 = 15
8	1	6	→ 8 + 1 + 6 = 15

2	4	9	2	4
+	+	+	+	+
5	3	5	7	5
+	+	+	+	+
8	8	1	6	6
=	=	=	=	=
15	15	15	15	15

In the Lo Shu square, all the numbers add up to 15, horizontally, vertically, and diagonally.

The number sigil wards off jealousy   133

The sigil of the Lo Shu is known as the Sigil of Saturn and it is regarded as a very aggressive symbol of protection against the ill effects of time. Basically the sigil looks like two love triangles facing each other with a line cutting through them at a ninety-degree angle. This face of the Lo Shu sigil is believed to have the power to ward off obstacles and ensure a smooth relationship between loved ones. It also effectively overcomes stressful jealousy from people watching your success and feeling envy arising within them. All successful people need protection against this sort of jealousy.

The Sigil is one of the more effective and potent remedies against this sort of aggravation.

The sigil is named after the planet Saturn.

The flight path of the Sigil of Saturn

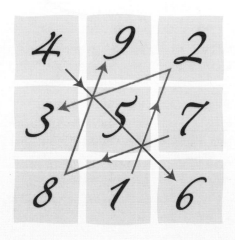

Note how the numbers move around the grid from one little square to the next. Two things may be observed here:

1. The numbers move alternately down and up from 5 to 6 to 7 to 8 and so forth, allowing a symbol to be formed from the pathway between the numbers. As the numbers move up and down this path way it reflects the way the chi energy moves up and down around a home, and it also reveals the nature of both luck and energy—that they are never static, always fluctuating, moving up and down.
2. In moving up and down, the numbers are in effect revealing a "flight path" for the way the numbers are supposed to move. It is this flight path that becomes the basis of one of feng shui's more potent formula methods—flying star feng shui. All feng shui charts are created by using the flight plan that originated in the Lo Shu square. But more than that, the Lo Shu square also reveals the Sigil of Saturn, which is believed to be an extremely powerful amulet of protection.

134 The Lo Shu number of the year

When we speak of the Lo Shu number we always talk about the center number of the Lo Shu square. Looked at another way: as long as one has the Lo Shu number, one can create the Lo Shu square because once the center number is filled in the remaining numbers can be placed correctly within the rest of the nine sector grids. All you need to do is follow the flight path of the original Lo Shu square, noting how the numbers move in ascending order around the nine sectors of the Lo Shu square.

Using this method of computation, it is then possible to create the Lo Shu chart for any given year—as long as you start with the Lo Shu number of the year, month, or even a single day. Whether year, month, or day, the Lo Shu number leads to the chart and from the chart one is able to discover the qualities of the timeframe in question.

How to plot a Lo Shu square for any year

1 Write the Lo Shu year number in the center square.

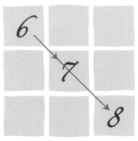

2 Place the numbers before and after the year number as shown.

3 The next number, 9, goes center right.

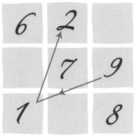

4 After 9, continue the sequence with 1 and 2 as shown.

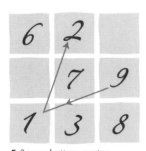

5 3 goes bottom center.

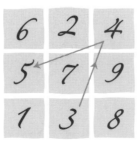

6 4 and 5 go as shown.

Your monthly lucky direction

People often ask me if there is any advantage to be gained by tracking the Lo Shu energy of time. My answer truthfully is, 'Yes!' If you have the time to do so, it is extremely beneficial to spare a few moments to go through your Lo Shu feng shui chart for the month. What the chart reveals is the location of every number from 1 to 9 in the house, which will indicate which direction is your personal one, so that you can find your lucky direction and location for the month.

From a practical viewpoint, it is not really necessary to investigate your Lo Shu number luck on a daily basis but it is definitely beneficial at the start of every year to check the Lo Shu number for the year and then create the relevant Lo Shu chart. This features strongly in the updating that everyone's living space requires.

A summary of all annual updates based on your animal sign is contained in my Fortune and Feng Shui books for each of the twelve animal signs, which are published annually. You can also see my website for the Lo Shu updates for the following year. Each year, if you wish to update your space, all you need is to go this website for the year in question to get all the information you need to successfully update your home.

Lo Shu charts for the month and year 135

All Lo Shu charts of the different months and for the year indicate the number that "rules" each of the eight outer sectors of a home. The meanings of the nine numbers stay the same as previously discussed. Thus the white numbers 1, 6, and 8 are said to be auspicious, while the misfortune numbers 2, 5, and 3 are not so good. The number 7 brings violence and burglary luck.

The annual Lo Shu chart becomes the feng shui chart of the year after additional information about other afflictions are placed within. You then use the chart to update your fortune and feng shui at the start of each year.

2010:	7	3	5
	6	8	1
	2	4	9

2011:	6	2	4
	5	7	9
	1	3	8

The central number on these charts indicates the Lo Shu year number, 8 for 2010 and 7 for 2011.

Significance of number combinations 136

Reading year and month combinations of numbers within the month and year charts reveals a great deal about the quality of each day, allowing you to decide whether a day is good or bad for you. Do this by using your animal sign or the location of your bedroom in the house; this is to check whether your astrological location or the room in which you sleep is being hit by a misfortune number or numbers.

Monthly readings of both houses and zodiac animal signs are very relevant to maintaining your good fortune, and for stronger readings I always encourage the combination of the monthly with the annual numbers.

These combinations that comprise the month and the year will accurately alert you to difficult times in the months ahead, from a variety of ills. For instance when month and year show the same center number then you know that good becomes better, but bad becomes worse!

Your Chinese animal sign, combined with month and year house charts, can warn you of good and bad fortune to come.

137 Combinations that bring abundance

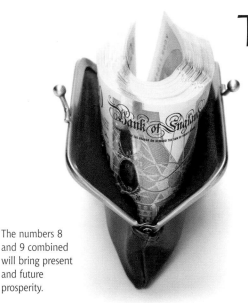

The 1,6, and 8 combinations in the charts always brings abundance, good fortune, and a pleasant harmonious time during the year. Any two-number combination here of these three white numbers is auspicious. In addition there are other groups of numbers to watch for when year and month charts are combined. Here are the auspicious combinations:

* 6 and 9 are auspicious and this enhances speculative luck
* 1 and 4 are auspicious, bringing the luck of good growth energy
* 8 and 9 are excellent as they signify present and future prosperity
* All sum-of-ten combinations are auspicious (1+9; 2+8 and so forth)
* All parent string specials—the three numbered combinations of 1, 4, 7, then 3, 6, 9, and 2, 5, 8—are excellent.

The numbers 8 and 9 combined will bring present and future prosperity.

138 Do not activate negative affliction numbers

A great way to practice defensive feng shui is to remember never to activate any of the negative numbers in your chart. Wherever they occur in your house they must not be inadvertently energized in any way whether through the presence of bright lights, windchimes, or music—all of which can cause them to "come alive." It is also advisable never to enhance a space that is already afflicted.

Instead, it is a good idea to suppress those parts of your home that are hurt by harmful afflictive numbers, using powerful feng shui cures. All negative causing numbers should always be strongly suppressed. This ensures the safety of residents and visitors to the house.

Remedies to counter negative affliction numbers

- The cure for the illness 2 star is metallic wu lous
- The cure for the misfortune star 5 is the five-element pagoda or bell
- The cure for the bloody 7 is the blue rhino, or elephant with its trunk raised.

Power of the Lo Shu specials—the sum of ten   139

T here are two special combinations of numbers that should be highlighted so that when you encounter them you become aware of them, and you can then energize them mentally to benefit from them. These are the numbers that make up the sum-of-ten and the numbers that make up the parent string of numbers.

The luck of these numbers is subtle but powerful, bringing together a complementary group of auspicious numbers. This applies especially to the sum-of-ten combinations, and they are collectively known as the Lo Shu specials. The way to use the sum-of-ten combination is to look at your lucky number. You can designate your lucky number by whichever method you wish—it can be your Birth Number, your Name Number, your Kua Number or your Taoist lucky number from your day of birth number... I have discovered that people have varying experiences when it comes to pinpointing the number that is genuinely lucky for them, the one that resonates with their inner chi energy.

Luck from the sum-of-ten

Once you know your lucky number then the number that creates a sum-of-ten combination with your lucky number brings completion luck for you, giving you the ability to bring all of your projects to fruition.

The sum-of-ten can also be a wealth-enhancing number. For instance, if 8 is your lucky number then creating the presence of 2 will be excellent, either as a house number or as a car number. Needless to say the combination of 2 and 8 is excellent during this period as these are the numbers that indicate the direct and indirect spirit of the current Period of 8. However, other sums of ten—4 and 6, 3 and 7, and 5 and 5—are also good although not as good as 2+8 and 1+9; the latter signifies present and future prosperity.

The parent string works the same way but here all three numbers must somehow be present so they can be seen as digits rather than numbers per se. The parent string combination overcomes many of the afflictions of feng shui.

The numbers 2 and 8, and 1 and 9 are particularly auspicious sum-of-ten combinations.

Chinese numerology as individual birth charts

You can enhance the power of the Lo Shu square by creating a personal chart based on your date of birth. See how the numbers of your birthday fit into the grid and then learn the significance of the various numbers, the importance of doubled numbers, and the meanings of the lines of numbers—as well as the lines that are completely missing.

Natal Lo Shu charts using your date of birth   143

In addition to using numbers to determine auspicious and inauspicious flows of energy within the environment, the Chinese science of numerology also taps one's date of birth to construct numerology charts that can reveal a great deal of information about an individual's tendency traits and how these affect their destiny over time. To the Chinese, numerology is always associated with the Lo Shu square, and we have seen that the numbers that fly around the Lo Shu change, transform, and engage with other numbers to reveal the quality of different kinds of luck and luck patterns. So, just as these can affect environments, they can also affect individuals.

To construct an individual's personalized chart, start by using the date of birth to fill in the different grids on the Lo Shu square. Here the dilemma is to decide whether to use one's lunar birth date or simply our birth date according to the Western, Gregorian calendar. I have actually tested this out for over fifteen years and have come to the conclusion that if the person whose chart I am creating uses the Western calendar, my findings using charts based on their Western calendar date of birth is actually a lot more accurate. This proves that it is perfectly possible to construct personal numerology natal charts using the date of birth according to the Western calendar.

The secret formula   144

How do you construct your personalized natal chart? First of all you must be familiar with the original Lo Shu square. Look at the numbers 1 to 9 in the square shown to the right and note that each digit is shown in its position in the original square, with the 5 at the center.

Now take your date of birth. Say you were born on January 5 1944. This means you were born on the 5th day of the 1st month, in the year 1944—written in numerology form this is 5.1.1944.

Now fill in the numbers of your birth date onto the Lo Shu chart as shown. Here is what the chart looks like. Some numbers—the 1 and the 4—appear more than once while many numbers (those shown in faint type) do not appear at all.

See how many times your birth date numbers appear on the Lo Shu chart.

Reading the chart

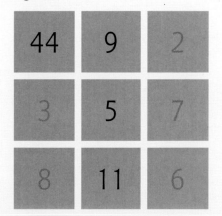

The first step in understanding your chart is to use all the numbers in your date of birth. Note that not all the grids have numbers from the birth date. There is, however, a double 4 in the southeast sector and a double 1 in the north sector. The center vertical is all filled while the right vertical grids do not contain any birth date numbers.

145 How to create a personal natal chart

Here are some more examples of how to create personalized natal charts. These are three examples of how to create the chart and also an idea of how to analyze the chart based on the way the numbers fit into the grid. In each case concentrate on the numbers shown in bold—the faint numbers represent the sectors of the Lo Shu square that are not filled.

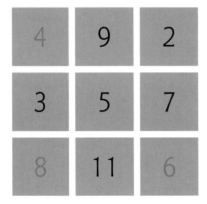

4	9	2
3	5	7
8	11	6

4	9	2
3	5	7
8	111	6

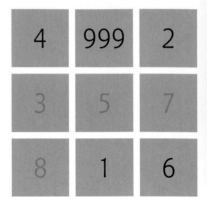

4	999	2
3	5	7
8	1	6

Date of birth: January 27 1953. In numbers this will be 1.27.1953

The chart here shows a double 1, the 5, and the 9 making the middle vertical line; and the 3, 5, and 7 making the middle horizontal line. As we shall see later, the vertical line of numbers indicates a balance of the material, the spiritual, and the intellectual planes. Here it is the middle line that is filled, also known as the line of willpower. This line, with the double 1 at the base, indicates determination to amass material things—the double 1 is an auspicious number because it symbolizes a good life and there is wealth indicated on the material plane. Having a double 1 in your chart is usually very auspicious.

Date of birth: October 16 1948. In numbers this will be 10.16.1948

This chart is extremely auspicious. The material plane here—the horizontal line at the bottom of the grid—has all three of the numbers 1, 6, and 8 represented, which is an indication of great prosperity. This line also suggests a practical, down-to-earth person to whom commercial success comes easily. The triple white numbers of 1,6, and 8 usually suggests great abundance. The other numbers in the grid, 4 and 9, are also the Ho Tu combination signifying the Fire element, which suggests that success is easy to come by. Here the middle horizontal line is completely missing, suggesting that this person is lacking in a spiritual dimension.

Date of birth: September 24 1969. In numbers this will be 9.24.1969

This is the chart of an intellectual with the triple 9 in the top horizontal line—probably someone who has found success in the judiciary or the legal profession. Put another way, if this person is a lawyer or in academia he will do extremely well. This is because the top horizontal line indicates the intellect, someone who is a good thinker and is also very skillful in putting his viewpoints across. The presence of the three 9s is excellent as the 9 expresses the fullness of heaven; it is a complete number and having it supported by side pillars 4 and 2 indicates a person of authority.

Reading the personalized natal chart 146

When empty the three horizontal and three vertical grids within the Lo Shu square—these nine spaces of equal size—represent a person who has not yet been born. Upon birth the numbers appear. Each of the numbers 1 to 9 will always occupy the same space no matter how often it occurs in the birth date, so the reading looks for the number of times each digit appears. The more times it is present the stronger its influence will be.

A full natal chart that has all nine numbers present signifies a perfect chart—and a perfect person—but such an occurrence is impossible of course, because a full birth date comprises a maximum of only eight numbers. Even if we add in the hour of birth there is only a remote possibility that all nine squares will be filled. A zero in the birth date is ignored because it is deemed to have no value in numerology. But it does have the effect of reducing the number of numerals appearing in the natal chart; in this way the 0 does have an indirect impact on the chart, and by extension on the personality and destiny of the person.

The nine squares represent the perfection of the universe and symbolize the three dimensions of existence. This means the mental or intellectual dimension, which is represented by the top horizontal grids; then the spiritual or emotional dimension across the middle horizontal grids, and finally the material or physical dimension across the bottom horizontal grids.

When a baby is born, his or her individual natal chart numbers appear.

The three levels of numbers

The numbers that occupy each of these dimensions suggest the attitude and personality of the person. Thus if the numbers emphasize the material dimension it indicates a tendency towards being practical and down to earth. The numbers in each of the three dimensions emphasizes the person's preferred forms of expression, his or her deepest motivations and subconscious inherent needs.

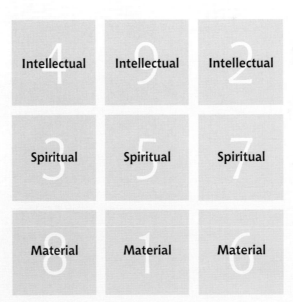

4 Intellectual	*9* Intellectual	*2* Intellectual
3 Spiritual	*5* Spiritual	*7* Spiritual
8 Material	*1* Material	*6* Material

The numbers are arranged into rows: intellectual, emotional or spiritual, and the material level.

147 The intellectual dimension

The numbers that run across the top line of the grid symbolize a person's intellectual capability and, to a large extent, they also reveal that person's ability to articulate his or her thoughts; when the sectors in this line are full it suggests someone who is very persuasive and is able to communicate very well. Usually when the top line of grids is not occupied by numbers it is likely that the person is not very talkative, or is usually not good at expressing himself or herself.

When the numbers here are present, however, note that there will be a 4, a 9, or a 2, which—if all are seen together—then signify the intellect of the person will be the dominant factor of their personality. When there is a predominance of 9s it suggests someone excellent at projecting himself or herself. When the 4 is present it suggests that the intellect is best

The top row of numbers relates to intellectual life.

The top row—the intellectual dimension

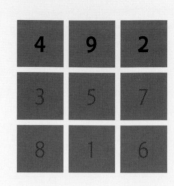

Think of the numbers in the top row as indicators of intellectual ability. To understand a person's character fully you should see how these numbers interact with the other numbers in their chart—in both the horizontal and vertical planes.

4	9	2
3	5	7
8	1	6

expressed through writing, but if the 2 dominates it suggests someone who is both creative and strategic in thinking.

The top line also resonates with a pronounced conscious awareness of the inner self, especially if combined with numbers appearing in the spiritual dimension—the 3, 5, and 7. And when combined with numbers on the material plane—the 8, 1, and 6—it indicates awareness of facts and figures pointing to someone who uses their intellect in a business context with some success.

If the all numbers from the other two dimensions are missing altogether—so that only the top row has numbers filled in—there is a very serious lack of balance in the chart; and this is not a very good indication at all. This might show a person who thinks too much, talks too much, or pontificates excessively.

The spiritual and emotional dimension   148

The center grid of numbers—3, 5, and 7—together represent the emotional nature of the personality—feelings, instincts, and intuition. This dimension of the self connects the intellect to the practical side of living.

These numbers suggest someone who is sensitive and tends to be more emotional than rational. Too many 5s will indicate the negative effects of being emotional—allowing oneself to get carried away by emotions—but a total absence of numbers in this dimension, however, might indicate a person who is cold and unfeeling.

Find the indication of good fortune

An excess of 3s points to a quarrelsome, fault-finding person who is easily angered; a single 3, though, is an indication of good fortune brought by someone whose spiritual dimension is at a good level. When there is also a 7 to create a sum of ten with the 3, the indications are also auspicious; but when there is an excess of 7s it indicates hard times.

If the numbers in the spiritual dimension are not balanced by at least some numbers in the other two line grids, they suggest someone who is completely ruled by the heart rather than by the head, led by feelings of obsession, anger, and hate. Only when there are numbers in the other grids can there be balance and the rise of true spirituality.

The center row—the spiritual dimension

4	9	2
3	**5**	**7**
8	1	6

The numbers of the spiritual dimension indicate a well-grounded personality—as long as they are accompanied by numbers from the other dimensions. Having numbers from a single line of the grid can be seriously unbalancing.

The material dimension   149

The bottom row—the material dimension

4	9	2
3	5	7
8	**1**	**6**

Although the numbers of the bottom row suggest a life of abundance, problems can arise if their power is not tempered by numbers from either the intellectual or spiritual dimensions.

The numbers 8, 1, and 6—either together or singly—are the prosperity numbers in Chinese numerology. These numbers represent commercial success, abundance, wealth, and financial gain, whether through your own business or while working for a company. But when there are too many of these numbers in the chart it can indicate excess. Too much opulence brings arrogance and egotism into the picture and these problems are often the result of having too much material success without the balance of either the intellectual or spiritual dimensions.

When the material dimension dominates the personalized natal chart, and there is a complete absence of numbers in the spiritual dimension, it suggests a personality that is cold and devoid of feelings, someone interested only in the pursuit of power and wealth. If the numbers in the intellectual plane are missing it suggests a rich person who could waste away his wealth or be easily cheated.

The material level represents material wealth.

150 Individual numbers in the Lo Shu chart

The meanings of the individual numbers or combination of numbers assists the practitioner to read the natal chart, but it is important to remember that under this system there is no ruling number to look for; instead the reading is based on the combined meanings of any of the nine numbers that are present. In addition the numbers also symbolize a host of things—elements, directions, and attributes—based on the Pa Kua and these can and should be factored into the reading.

Also when reading the chart, it is the way the numbers combine that appear to offer deeper insights so while individual numbers are studied, it

If the numbers for your home are inauspicious, you can consider using "remedies" based on the theory of the five elements.

Reading the natal chart

Do not stop at interpreting the individual numbers of planes of your natal chart, study it so that you can see its full meaning.

You can also boost parts of the chart that are missing with other feng shui cures. If your chart is missing one number from a line you can make up for it by invoking that number's related color or element in your home or wardrobe.

is just as important to look at the way the numbers combine. The explanations of each of the numbers are not exhaustive, especially in the depth of the various permutations. Readers are strongly urged to use what is given as tendencies rather than read them as absolutes, or unalterable facts. Also remember that there is a positive and a negative aspect to every number.

Use elements to boost your numbers

When the indication appears inauspicious, you can consider using "remedies" based on the theory of the five elements. If an auspicious number that would "improve the chart" is missing then check for the corresponding element and surround yourself with it. For instance, if the 6 is missing, and its presence would add to the 1 and 8 already present, then what is needed is Metal element as 6 is signified by Metal. So wearing gold would be very helpful in making up for the missing 6.

If, say, the number 3 is missing and you want it to make an auspicious Ho Tu combination with the 8 in your chart, then wearing green would be most helpful since this is the color of 3. The properties and attributes of the nine numbers in a natal chart context are covered in the next pages.

The number 1 in your chart   151

Located in the center of the material dimension, the number 1 expresses a person's practical nature and his concern over things material and physical. This is by itself an auspicious number because it generally indicates someone whose lifestyle is comfortable.

A single 1 in the grid suggests a person with average riches. If the 6 and 8 are also present the combination is said to be extremely lucky. If the other two numbers are missing, a single one in the material plane indicates someone who is comfortable in their life but there is no great wealth in the person's destiny.

Note that 1 and 6 is a Ho Tu combination bringing good fortune; while 1 and 9 is a sum-of-ten, which is also a indicator of good prospects for material wealth.

Two 1s is better than a single 1. Their presence indicates prosperity in small doses and, again, when combined with 6 and 8 it indicates a rich and good life. When two 1s combine with the 4 it brings love affairs into your life, so you will need to be ready to incorporate the emotional plane of your natal chart.

Three 1s denote a very happy person—someone who has plenty to smile about. This is a person whose material needs are always met and

whose disposition attracts rich and successful people into his or her life. When it sits alongside the 6 and the 8, the material wealth luck it generates is phenomenal.

If four 1s are present, though, they are always interpreted as an excessive concentration, suggesting an obsession with the pursuit of wealth that can turn negative, dominating all other aspects of your life—especially if there are missing numbers in the spiritual dimension. If the 6 and 8 are present they do suggest the person is not lacking emotionally, but with so many 1s the imbalance can be too severe.

Please note that the number of 1s in a natal chart does not necessarily indicate degree of financial success. It does give a comfort level—usually three 1s is the best indicator of good fortune. People with three 1s are usually excellent communicators and are able to become commercially successful using the power of speech.

A single number 1 in your chart on the material plane suggests average wealth.

4	9	2
3	5	7
8	**1**	6

1 and 6 is a Ho Tu combination, bringing good fortune.

152 The number 2 in your chart

4	9	**2**
3	5	7
8	1	6

The number 2 exists on the intellectual plane.

The number 2 is the third number of the intellectual dimension and is commonly seen as an indicator of both rational or irrational thinking. It is the most common number found in birth dates, appearing 50 to 60% of the time—and from the year 2000 onward it will appear in everyone's chart.

When the 2 appears with the other numbers of the intellectual dimension—9 and 4—the combination suggests a strong intellect. Such people often have distinguished careers in academia, research, and also in the literary and writing professions.

A single 2 standing on its own without the 4 or 9 suggests a mediocre mind—this is someone who requires guidance and is more of a follower than a leader. Amongst the intellectual numbers the number 2 is the weakest indicator of intellect so it is not highly rated as an intellectual number unless the 9 is present, in which case a Ho Tu combination is formed and this is an auspicious indication. The numbers 2 and 9 in the same chart suggest fame and fortune arising from one's creativity and intellectual prowess. There can be success in the judiciary and legal professions, too. Combined with 4, there might be some success in the media.

When the single 2 combines with a 5 or an 8 it strengthens the Earth element in the chart so, if Earth benefits the person, then the combination is a good one. Combined with 8 it is excellent because not only is 8 of the current period, and is thus a lucky number, but with the 2 the sum-of-ten is created, which is excellent and lucky.

Luck of combined 2s

If two 2s combine with the 9 and the 4 the result is regarded as lucky, and this is the same with the 5

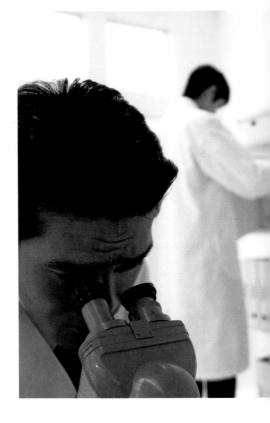

and the 8. However a double 2 can also emphasize the negative side of the number.

Three 2s is definitely troublesome and unless balanced by numbers in the other dimensions—especially the lucky numbers 1,6, or 8—so many 2s in the natal chart can suggest a vulnerability to illness. You will need Metal energy from the 6 and 7 to remedy the situation.

Four 2s is a huge imbalance, which can lead to severe illness or arrogance. They need to be balanced with the Metal numbers 6 and 7 or they could burst through as bad temper, sarcasm, and hostility towards others, which can bounce back as harm. People with too many 2s are often impatient and also tend to react badly to situations causing misunderstandings in their life.

The number 3 in your chart   153

Three is the first number of the spiritual dimension, symbolizing intuition and good feelings. It is a barometer of your emotional well-being and strength. The 3 is a reliable guide to the degree of sensitivity and intuition you apply to all your affairs. However, an absence of 3 in the chart does not indicate an absence of feelings, just as plenty of 3s do not indicate a high intuitive level. Much of Chinese numerology is to do with balance—too much of any number is not necessarily a good thing.

A single 3 suggests a degree of sensitivity and intuition that is not adequate to cope with highly competitive situations, unless combined with the other two numbers—5 and 7—of the horizontal spiritual plane, or with the 4 and 8 in the vertical line that indicates a planner. People who have the 3 but not the 5 or 7 are often the victims of emotional distress, getting their feelings hurt and suffering from heartaches.

The number 3 and 5 indicates love sickness but if the 3 combines with the 8 to form a Ho Tu combination, a protective shoulder is created. People with a single 3 in their natal chart should avoid high-stress jobs.

Two 3s are people whose sensitivity and intuition are better balanced. They are blessed with high intelligence and their innate understanding of people and situations bring success to them. Such people are also good at sniffing our false friends—they place a high level of importance on trustworthiness and they themselves make good friends. A chart that combines the 3 with the 5 and 7 indicates someone who is spiritually inclined.

Three 3s denote hypersensitive people. Immersed in their own world, such people tend to get cut off from the rest of the world so they can be very out of touch with contemporary trends, unless this factor is balanced by the presence of the 5 and 7. Four 3s people are impatient and unreliable.

4	9	2
3	5	7
8	1	6

Number 3 exists on the emotional and spiritual plane.

154 The number 4 in your chart

4	9	2
3	5	7
8	1	6

Number 4 relates to the rational, thinking part of the brain.

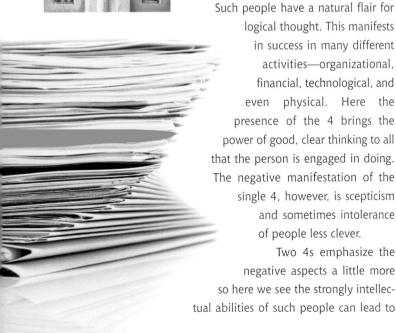

Symbolically the number 4 represents the rational aspects of the intellectual dimension. People with this number in their natal chart are logical, meticulous, and are usually highly disciplined in their approach to life. But they tend to have a low tolerance level to those who are less intellectual than they are.

Readers should not get confused about the meaning of 4. Conventional superstition has always assigned an inauspicious meaning to the number 4, mainly because the phonetics of 4 in many Chinese dialects sounds like the word death, hence some consider it an unlucky number.

In the Lo Shu system of numerology, however, the number 4 has lucky and positive connotations. In the natal chart a single 4 indicates a person whose mental capability is good and this is because the number 4 is the anchor number of the Lo Shu square's intellectual dimension.

Such people have a natural flair for logical thought. This manifests in success in many different activities—organizational, financial, technological, and even physical. Here the presence of the 4 brings the power of good, clear thinking to all that the person is engaged in doing. The negative manifestation of the single 4, however, is scepticism and sometimes intolerance of people less clever.

Two 4s emphasize the negative aspects a little more so here we see the strongly intellectual abilities of such people can lead to

The number 4 in a natal chart indicates intellectual rigor, clear thinking, and excellent organizational skills.

intolerance and impatience. If there are numbers in the spiritual dimension to balance, then the negative aspects of impatience will get reduced. Three 4s suggest even greater difficulty in getting along with people who are less clever, dynamic, or intellectual than you. It's called looking down on people, and is a negative trait that ultimately brings downfall.

The number 5 in your chart   155

The number 5 has a special position in the center of the chart where it governs the intensity of human feelings. It is the second number in the spiritual dimension and it exerts a very strong influence on the power and passion of emotions. It also gives strength of resolution when present in anyone's natal chart. With the 5 in your chart you can take action, initiate projects, and make things happen. So the 5 brings underlying strength to your levels of determination and this is because a single 5 in a natal chart brings balanced emotional control.

People who have it often possess good and reliable instincts when making judgments, so decisions tend to be solid and well thought out. They will make fewer mistakes caused by giving in to unthinking emotion-driven reactions. But negative aspects of 5 can emerge and when these occur the result tends to be unhappy—negative 5 rears its head when there are 2s or 3s in the chart. If these numbers do not occur in the chart, the single 5 person will demonstrate a strength of character that is quite extraordinary in its effect on the life destiny. So, from this viewpoint, a single 5 is viewed as something very positive indeed. It is like rising to the occasion when a golden opportunity comes along and making something ordinary quite extraordinary.

Two 5s people can frequently demonstrate an intense inner fervor and passion; you can sometimes recognize them by their powerful eyes and furrowed brows. Intense determination gives them an air of confidence and self-assurance which, if supported by the numbers 1 and 9, demonstrate a formidable combination. Such people often succeed in attaining great heights of achievement.

Beware the double 5

The negative aspects of the double 5 are manifested in a tendency towards arrogance. People can be insufferable and unbearable with their "know it all" attitudes. There is a danger that there is too much energy inside and if there is no outlet such people can turn to other forms for expressing their drive and intensity. That is when the energy can become dangerous, especially when the outlet for expressing the energy is negative—excessive indulgences in things like drugs, sex, or even violence. This is the negative side of the 5 and it can be dangerous.

Three 5s have too much power and most people cannot handle it—fortunately few are born with this degree of intensity in their feelings. When present, however, discipline must be learnt from a very young age.

Number 5 governs intensity and action.

4	9	2
3	**5**	7
8	1	6

156 The number 6 in your chart

The number 6 symbolically represents satisfaction in a material sense. On its own, this auspicious number and its location in the bottom horizontal of the chart emphasizes the practical aspects of existence. If you have a 6 you are likely to have a comfortable life. Financially you will not be lacking and there will always be a steady flow of income into your life.

A single 6 indicates a person who possesses the good fortune to enjoy monetary luck. It is a very good number when it appears with the 8 and the 1 on the horizontal line since this then forms the powerful combination of white numbers 1,6, and 8. But if the other two numbers are not in the chart, the 6 will bring about manifestation of good luck through the creativity of the individual.

4	9	2
3	5	7
8	1	**6**

The number 6 brings material satisfaction.

The creativity of the 6

People with the single 6 love creating and decorating their homes. They have a special skill in establishing harmony and happiness within a domestic context. As they mature they will become more affluent and there will always be people to help them. The Chinese describe this kind of luck as having affinity with mankind.

Two 6s represent the doubling of the creative power that can be utilized, but it can also lead to negative outcomes unless some the numbers of the center line—3, 5, or 7—are present to balance out the energies. Should the center line numbers be missing the person will be sensitive to temporary setbacks and become too needy of encouragement.

Three 6s suggest worries on the home front and these anxieties tend to be exaggerated in the mind and seem very real—and the worries usually revolve around material things, or the imagined lack thereof. This is never so marked when the 1 or 8 are also present in the chart.

The number 7 in your chart   157

This number is located on the horizontal spiritual dimension of the Lo Shu grid. As it was also last period's auspicious number its energy has slowed down. However, the number 7 represents a special perspective of the human experience and its broader meanings are often associated with the metaphysical aspects of existence. It symbolizes the soul of the person and suggests a deeper search for the meaning of life.

If you have a single 7 in your chart you will find that as you go into your forties you will become increasingly interested in things spiritual. Those who also have numbers in the material plane—1, 8, or 6—will find that they combine well with the 7, because a good balance is created between the materialistic and the spiritual aspects of the individual's existence.

When the bottom horizontal numbers are missing, and 7 combines with 3 and 5 instead, the person will be interested more in spiritual pursuits than in material gains. If there are too many of these numbers the individual will tend to be rather supercilious and self-righteous and if these numbers are repeated the self-righteousness tends to be dogmatic. Number 7 people tend to think of themselves as perfectionists.

Profound and attractive

Two 7s suggest someone whose approach to life is colored by philosophical underpinnings—they will rationalize about the soul and be attracted to all things they consider "deep" and profound. They are not easy individuals to get along with as their heads are usually high up in the clouds.

When the 7 is present and there are also numbers on all three of the other horizontal levels then the destiny of the person becomes very attractive, with success being well balanced. When the negative side prevails the individual views success with a guilt complex, and is then unable to savor their life to the full. This underlying guilt complex is the main drawback of the number 7 person. Hence anyone with three 7s in their chart usually finds themselves weighed down by ambivalence and a depressive state of mind.

The fullest negative arises when all the diagonal numbers 4, 5, and 6 are missing. This creates the poison arrow of scepticism whose ill effects are compounded by the presence of too many 7s. If this describes your chart you need to use the presence of Water as a remedy.

4	9	2
3	5	**7**
8	1	6

Number 7s find their spirituality during their 40s.

158 The number 8 in your chart

4	9	2
3	5	7
8	1	6

This is a very favorable number, which creates waves of good fortune. Its lucky connotations have to do with its premier position in the chart and also because it is the number of the current period—as a result it is at the height of its strength and power. Intrinsically 8 is a lucky number under almost any circumstances

A single 8 looks like a double four—that is one square above another—which elevates everything that is positive about the number 4. Here we see the hidden presence of the square which is also the symbol of Earth, the element of the number 8. The square has always represented balance and meticulous efficiency in all areas of living. When 8 combines with 6 and 1, they form the horizontal prosperity line spelling amazing good fortune. The presence of the 8 always adds to the good fortune of the individual, so it does suggest that anyone with the 8 present in the chart will have a reasonably comfortable life.

The 8 also looks like the infinity sign, which is, of course, the sign of never-ending good fortune. Multiplied three times the infinity becomes the mystical cross, so the symbolic connotations of 8 are most auspicious.

Number 8 is extremely lucky on every level, especially as we are living in the feng shui Period of 8.

Multiple 8s indicate business strength

Two 8s indicate sharpened power of the number—and it is an extremely beneficial indication. People with the double 8 are sure to excel in the commercial world. They succeed as business people and they usually make good trade judgments and are also able to take advantage of all opportunities that come their way.

The negative side of 8s surface when there are three or more 8s, and here is where the balance has been tilted allowing the 8's bad features to rear their ugly heads. Too many 8s spell over-confidence and arrogance. There is also the pursuit of material gain without consideration for the softer values, when the pursuit of success overrides all other considerations. Individuals with a surplus of material line numbers like 8 tend to pursue materialistic gains to the exclusion of all things. The resulting imbalance can cause unhappiness, unless a real effort is made to create better balance. Three 8s is definitely too much of a good thing so it is a good thing that this is not a common occurrence.

Some number 8 people see its presence as a sign of good fortune.

The number 9 in your chart   159

This is the number that symbolizes the fullness of heaven and earth. The 9 is also the number of future prosperity so its presence in the chart is both auspicious and exciting. Everyone born in the previous millennium has the 9 in their chart, indicating people who still had vestiges of idealism. Younger people born after 2000 do not necessarily have 9s in their charts, nevertheless the power of 9 in this early part of the 21st century continues...

People who possess a single 9 in their natal charts are usually clever, ambitious, and very self-assured. They will have success in academic and legal professions and they usually have authority and power over others. Judges and magistrates usually do well if they have at least one 9 in their charts. As do politicians and business leaders.

4	9	2
3	5	7
8	1	6

Number 9s are intellectual and idealistic.

Intellectual and idealistic

The double 9 is a sign of intellectual ability with a love for, and a respect for, learning. The double 9 is also an expression of idealism coupled with serious thought. These people tend to be deep thinkers who usually excel in professions requiring such attributes. Double 9 people tend to be level headed and pride themselves on their sense of fair play. They are ruled by their heads more than by their emotions, unless of course they are combined with an excess of the middle numbers 3, 5, or 7.

Three 9s in a chart suggest extreme idealism, which can be negative as it can manifest as intolerance. At its worst, it suggests a person with a very short fuse—a person with a quick and fiery temper. So three 9s is usually not a good indication to find in a chart.

160 Three numbers combination

In interpreting the numbers in the chart, note that one of the major guidelines of interpretation comes from the presence of any three numbers creating a straight line. These three numbers in a row reveal personality traits of significance and they offer important illumination into the inner self of the individual. They also indicate a potential direction of where destiny can lead to.

When three spaces in any row are empty, they are also factored into the reading since these lines—known as arrows—indicate weaknesses or negative attributes.

Hence when we refer to three numbers combinations, these are generally referring to the presence or absence of three numbers forming a straight line. These can be vertical, or horizontal, or the line of numbers that is missing might also be diagonal.

Most people have at least one arrow representing a significant weakness in their character. When there are two or more arrows, it is an indication of a person who has a very strong character or is stubborn. Having said that, it is more beneficial to read the full lines of numbers.

Full line combinations

There are three vertical, three horizontal lines, and two diagonal lines possible so a natal chart may have 8 full lines. As for lines with empty spaces there are five possibilities amongst those born in the last century (since every natal chart from the year 1900 to 1999 will include the 1 and the 9). This means that amongst the world's population there is still potentially more possibilities for strength from full number lines, than for weaknesses from the empty spaces that create invisible arrows in the chart.

161 Lines of determination and willpower

The line of determination is the diagonal line made up of the numbers 8, 5, and 2. All are Earth numbers that, when they occur together in the chart, are a strong indication of persistence, willpower, and great determination. Determination underscores this person's every action and—coupled with sheer persistence—individuals having this line of numbers demonstrate great resilience in the face of setbacks, disappointments, and even failure. This is a person who will always come back for a rematch should he or she lose, and will continue trying until they succeed.

This is a person who will bide his or her time, wait out a bad period, and ultimately try again until success happens. This is quite a formidable line of numbers to have because it suggests a resilience that is steadfast and unrelenting.

Meanwhile the line of willpower is indicated by the numbers 9, 5 and 1 in the vertical center line. Anyone born in the 1950s has this line and those who have it have a strong stubborn streak of resilience that can be very formidable. At its most positive, this line of numbers indicates endurance against great odds; persistence and resilience. At its worst, it suggests someone dogmatic and unyielding—but it also indicates the potential to rise to great heights of responsibility. You can have a great career as a politician as your tough endurance attributes make a suitable person to hold high office without fear or favor.

8, 5, 2 reveals determination.

4	9	**2**
3	**5**	7
8	1	6

Line of spirituality 162

The horizontal line comprising the numbers 3, 5, and 7 is the line of spirituality. We have already touched on this horizontal line of numbers, which emphasizes the emotions as well as the spiritual side of the individual. When these numbers are present in your chart, you will find that, as you grow older and mature, you begin to become increasingly fascinated with the spiritual side of life and you will also develop interests in the more esoteric sciences or even physics.

When this line of numbers is present you will take your search for the "meaning of life" very seriously. You will be drawn to contemplative pursuits, and meditations will be something almost all of you will engage in during later years. If, on the other hand, this line of numbers is missing, you will tend to be impatient with spirituality.

3, 5, and 7 shows spirituality.

4	9	2
3	**5**	**7**
8	1	6

Line of emotional balance 163

This is the diagonal 4, 5, 6 line and when these numbers are present in your chart you will display a natural balance in your emotional make up. You are spiritual and charitable but not in an extreme fashion. This is a wonderful line to have as it indicates someone with great sensitivity and understanding; someone whose awareness of other people's viewpoints makes them tolerant and easy to get on with. People with this line of numbers make excellent counselors, diplomats, teachers and motivators. They also find success in the healing professions.

This line is also indicative of people who are practical and well grounded in their attitude towards others. They do not have absurd expectations of their loved ones, friends, or colleagues and they are also down to earth and practical. But they have a depth of feelings which sometimes others cannot understand. Nevertheless, there is little danger of offending them because such people have a high tolerance level.

4	9	2
3	**5**	7
8	1	**6**

4, 5, and 6 show emotional balance.

164   Line of intellect

4	9	2
3	5	7
8	1	6

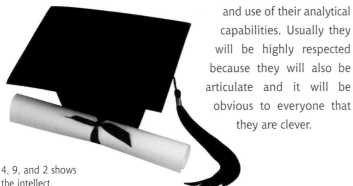

4, 9, and 2 shows the intellect.

The presence of the three numbers 4, 9, and 2 on the mental dimension of the Lo Shu natal chart emphasizes the dominance of the intellectual activity of the person. He or she will have great academic capability, good memory and be quite formidable in their demonstration of logic and use of their analytical capabilities. Usually they will be highly respected because they will also be articulate and it will be obvious to everyone that they are clever.

They will also have a preference for intellectual type pursuits and are happiest when stimulating their mind. There is thus a tendency to avoid, ignore, or belittle social situations that engage in what might be considered mindless pursuits, preferring the company of others whose mental capabilities are equally vigorous. People with this line of numbers usually avoid emotionally charged situations, being uncomfortable in situations when excessive emotion is displayed. They can be snobbish about their intellectual capability and often cannot suffer fools.

When this line of numbers is absent there is a tendency to be mentally lazy, often with a reluctance to use the mind. As a result these people might come across as being mentally challenged.

165   Line of prosperity

4	9	2
3	5	7
8	1	6

8, 1, and 6 reveals prosperity.

The line of numbers that indicate prosperity is the bottom horizontal 8, 1, 6 combination. All charts that possess these three numbers can rest assured that their life will be one of comfort and ease. Money, or the lack of it, will rarely be a problem and success is also easy to come by. You are also commercially minded, practical, and you love material possessions. Your pursuit of wealth is motivated by worldly desires.

The good thing about these material numbers is that they often combine well with other numbers on either the emotional or intellectual dimensions. But when these other numbers are missing there will be a surplus of the "lucky" 1, 6, 8 numbers and that is when attitudes become unbalanced, which is when outcomes can begin to become negative.

Line of the planner 166

When we look at the vertical lines we see first the vertical line of the planner, whose numbers comprise 4, 3 and 8. Planning in a Chinese sense suggest someone who is politically savvy, cunning, crafty, and shrewd—someone who painstakingly plans out every possible scenario and outcome.

This is the line of the natural politician, because they will have built-in antennas that alert them to possible outcomes in everything they do. It is also the line of professionals who work in large organizations, or in the army. When there are also the lines of the intellect present, this person can rise to a very high position of authority. The line of the planner supports those whose chart also includes the prosperity numbers.

4, 3, and 8 reveals those who like planning and are strategists.

4	9	2
3	5	7
8	1	6

Line of action 167

This is the vertical line that comprises the numbers 2, 7, and 6 and it indicates someone who is action oriented. The line combines the most expressive aspects of the three dimensions of intellect, emotion, and practicality.

If you have these three numbers in your chart, it means that you are always on the move. There is always something going on in your life and you express yourself through your activities. You will find that you are engaged in many different things at the same time and you will tend to overcommit your time to a large variety of causes.

People with this line of numbers tend to be successful sportsmen. They are very physical and usually love exercise and they look after their bodies. When combined with either the line of

2, 7, and 6 denote action-driven people.

4	9	2
3	5	7
8	1	6

determination or the line of will power we see a formidable combination, which can lead to success of immense significance—especially if there are no other numbers present in the chart to distract attention from them.

168 Arrows of suspicion, loneliness, frustrations, apathy, and confusion

Arrows in the chart suggest some negativity, and they are present when there are empty lines with no numbers present. Thus the arrow of suspicion is indicated by the missing numbers in the diagonal line containing 4-5-6. This is a person who does not trust others. You are naturally suspicious, cynical and skeptical. The missing numbers suggest an emptiness in your world view of people. You will worry too much and have difficulty letting people into your life. When you are hit by this arrow, it is a good idea to light up the center of the home with a bright light as it can help you overcome your naturally suspicious nature.

Arrow of suspicion

The arrow of loneliness is indicated by the missing line of numbers 3-5-7—the horizontal line in the middle of the chart. When you are hit by this arrow it means your life is seriously lacking in genuine good friends. There is also insufficient laughter in your life. Even when you attain success you will be blind to the joys of social interface, or to the comradeship of shared rejoicing. To counter this terrible lack in your life also shine a bright light in the center of the home. This will break the arrow of loneliness very efficiently.

Arrow of loneliness

Other inauspicious arrows

If the diagonal line of numbers 2-5-8 is missing it creates the arrow of frustration, which will cause blocks in your life, setbacks, and obstacles. There is the sadness of unfulfilled dreams when these numbers are completely missing. Disappointments can relate to love, to work, to failure in almost anything. Generally this arrow brings a blow to the spirit and the best way to overcome it is to hang a bright light in the center of the home. This is one of

Arrow of frustration

The arrows in Chinese numerology are figurative, showing in a natal chart areas of difficult or concern.

the best cures possible for arrows that cause unhappiness and frustrations.

There are two other arrows, that of apathy—caused by the missing numbers 2-7-6 on the right vertical—and the arrow of confusion—caused by the missing numbers 4-3-8 on the left vertical. When the numbers 2-7-6 are completely missing, you will suffer

Arrow of apathy

from an inability to get started or take advantage of opportunities that come your way. There is a lack of energy and spirit so that you are always putting off doing things that need to be done. Prevarication is the ruling attitude and it is not conducive to success. The cure for this is to hang wind chimes in the west sector of the home.

When the numbers 4-3-8 are totally missing, there is a lack of organization or clear thinking. Such people also cannot seem to make decisions or put down roots. They lack ambition and often find it hard to overcome lethargy in their lives. There is a heaviness that seems to prevent them from taking action. This arrow of confusion is overcome by planting a sturdy tree in the east. This is akin to establishing a strong foundation, which will override the lack of numbers in this part of the chart.

Arrow of confusion

Index

Picture credits

5 Left: Reflexstock/ Westend61/Achim Sass. Right: Reflexstock/Image Source. 6 Reflexstock/ Panthermedia Basic/Ignacio Gonzalez Prado.
7 Bottom right: Reflexstock/NFZ/lin suying.
8 Top: Reflexstock/NFZ/Lai Leng Yiap. Bottom: Reflexstock/ NFZ/Alvin Teo. 9 Getty Images/Peter Cade. 12 Reflexstock/PhotoNonStop/Hervé Gyssels/Photononstop. 13 Top: Loupe Images/ Sandra Lane. Bottom: Reflexstock/NFZ/Ablestock Premium. 14 Top: Getty Images/Ann Cutting.15 Top: Reflexstock/ PhotoAlto/ Michele Constantini. Bottom: Getty Images/Steve Smith.16 Bottom: Getty Images. 17 Top: Reflexstock/Glow Images. 18 Right: Getty Images/David Deas. 19 Top: Reflexstock/Westend61. Bottom: Reflexstock/ Image Source. 20 Bottom: Reflexstock/Fancy.
21 Left: Reflexstock/NFZ. Bottom right: Getty Images/The Bridgeman Art Library. 22 Bottom: Getty Images/Fry Design Ltd. 23 Top: Getty Images/Dimitri Vervitsiotis. Bottom: Reflexstock/ Corbis. 24 Top: Reflexstock/Aflo Score. Bottom: Reflexstock/Superstock. 25 Bottom: Reflexstock.
26 Top: Reflexstock. Bottom: Reflexstock/ Moodboard. 27 Top: Getty Images/Philip and Karen Smith. Bottom: Getty Images. 28 Getty Images/Laurence Dutton. 29 Getty Images/Dorling Kindersley. 30 Reflexstock/Imagebroker. 32 Top: Getty Images/Alistair Berg. Bottom: Reflexstock/ Corbis .33 Top: Reflexstock/ Tetra/PT Images. Bottom: Reflexstock/Fancy/Laura Doss. 34 Top: Reflexstock/ Superstock/Anton Vengo. Bottom: Reflexstock/Stock Connection/ Visions of America, LLC. 35 Bottom left: Reflexstock/Fancy/Lou Cypher. 36 Top: Getty Images/Philippe Gelot. Bottom: Reflexstock. 38 Left: Reflexstock/Image Source. Right: Reflexstock/Panthermedia Basic/Stefan Kriegel. 39 Left: wofs.com. Top right: Reflexstock/ Stefan Auth. Bottom right: Reflexstock/NFZ/lin suying. 40 Top left: Reflexstock/Stock Connection/ View Stock. Top right: Reflexstock/Tetra. Bottom: Reflexstock/Panthermedia Basic/Hsing-wen Hsu. 41 Left: Reflexstock/ BlendRF/Colln Anderson. Right: Reflexstock/Look Foto/Karl Johaentges/ LOOK-foto. 42 Top: Reflexstock/Look Foto/Karl Johaentges/LOOK-foto. Middle left: Reflexstock/ NFZ/Kae Horng Mau. Middle: Reflexstock/ heritage/The Museum of East Asian Art/Heritage-Images. Bottom middle: Reflexstock/heritage/The Museum of East Asian Art/Heritage-Images. Bottom right: Reflexstock/ NFZ/Bartlomiej Magierowski. 43 Top: Getty Images/ Glowimages. Bottom: Reflexstock/NFZ/Yenty Jap. 44 Left: Getty Images/Peter Cade. Right: Reflexstock/ Corbis. 45 Top: Reflexstock/Roberto Soncin Gerometta/Lonely Planet Images. Bottom: Reflexstock/NFZ/realname. 46 Top: Photolibrary/ Best View Stock. Bottom: Reflexstock/Look Foto/Ulli Seer. 47 Top: Getty Images/By Oki. Middle: Getty Images. Bottom: Reflexstock/NFZ /ping han. 49 Top: Getty Images/Marcus Mok. Bottom: Reflexstock/Axiom Photographic/Toby Adamson. 51 wofs.com. 52 Top: Getty Images/ Brian Hagiwara. Bottom: Reflexstock/Ken Seet/Corbis. 53 Left: Reflexstock.

54 Top: Reflexstock/First Light/Jo-Ann Richards. Bottom: Reflexstock/Fstop. 55 Top: Reflexstock/ Corbis. Bottom: Reflexstock/Fancy/Kate Kunz.
56 Top: Reflexstock/Corbis. 57 Reflexstock/ Narratives/Viv Yeo. 58 Top: Reflexstock/ Aflo Diversion/Yoshio Tomii Photo Studio. Bottom: Reflexstock/Ingram Publishing. 60 Top: Getty Images/Grant Faint. 61 Top: Getty Images/John Foxx. Bottom: Reflexstock/Corbis. 62 Left: Getty Images/Lew Robertson. Right: Reflexstock/Photo Alto. 63 Reflexstock/Image Source. 66 Top: Reflexstock/NFZ/bram janssens. Bottom: Reflexstock/Lawrence Manning/Corbis. 67 Top: Getty Images/Dimitri Vervitsiotis. 68 Reflexstock/ Vivant/pepperprint. 69 Top: Getty Images/Philip and Karen Smith. 70 Top: Getty Images/Burazin. 72 Top: Reflexstock/NFZ/Kheng Ho Toh. Middle: Reflexstock/ NFZ/Tatiana Popova. Bottom: Reflexstock/NFZ/Anton Hlushchenko. 74 Reflexstock/NFZ/Benjamin Albiach Galan. 75 Top: Reflexstock/First Light/Jo-Ann Richards. 76 Reflexstock/NFZ/Lai Leng Yiap. 77 Getty Images/ Gert Tabak. 78 Reflexstock/ NFZ/Anne Kitzman. 79 Top: Reflexstock/NFZ/Anne Kitzman. Bottom: Reflexstock. 80 Reflexstock/NFZ/Kheng Ho Toh. 81 Getty Images/redcover.com. 82 Left: Reflexstock/ Johner RF/Andreas Kindler. Right: Reflexstock. 83 Reflexstock/NFZ/Aleksandr Kurganov. 85 Top: Reflexstock/NFZ/Aleksey Puris. Bottom: Getty Images/Thomas Northcut. 86 Top: Loupe Images, ph Chris Everard/the London apartment of the Sheppard Day Design Partnership (www.sheppard-day.com). Bottom: Reflexstock/ NFZ/Shariff Che'Lah. 87 Middle: wofs.com. Bottom: Reflexstock/ NFZ/ Kheng Guan Toh. 88 Reflexstock/Corbis. 89 Top: Reflexstock/ Moodboard. Bottom: Reflexstock/ heritage/The Museum of East Asian Art/Heritage-Images. 90 Top: Reflexstock/NFZ/Kheng Ho Toh. Bottom: Getty Images/Bill Ling. 91 Top: Reflexstock/PhotoNonStop/Sarramon-Cardinale. Bottom: Reflexstock/Image Source. 94 Top: Reflexstock/First Light/Yves Marcoux. 95 Reflexstock/NFZ/realname. 97 Top: Loupe Images. Bottom: Loupe Images. 98 Reflexstock/NFZ/ Flavia Morlachetti. 99 Loupe Images. 100 Top: Loupe Images. Bottom: Reflexstock/Tetra/ Jamie Grill. 101 Reflexstock/Stock Connection/Peter Gridley. 102 Top: Cico Books/Roy Palmer. Bottom: Reflexstock/NFZ/Marat Utimishev. 103 Left: Reflexstock/Westend61/Nico Hermann. Top right: Reflexstock/FStop. Middle and bottom right: Cico Books/Roy Palmer. 104 Top: Reflexstock/Greer & Associates, Inc. / SuperStock. Bottom: Reflexstock/ Panthermedia Basic/Halil Ertem.105 Top: Reflexstock/NFZ/Alvin Ganesh Balasubramaniam. 106 Top: Reflexstock/Johner RF/Mikael Dubois. Bottom: Reflexstock/ Westend61/Andreas Koschate. 107 Top: Loupe Images. Bottom: Reflexstock/Radius Images. 108 Reflexstock/ Flint/Corbis. 109 Reflexstock/Stock Connection/ Peter Gridley. 110 Reflexstock/PhotoNonStop/ Eric Audras. 113 Top: Reflexstock/Rubberball/ Nicole Hill. Bottom:

Reflexstock/Radius Images. 114 Top: Reflexstock/ NFZ/Kheng Ho Toh. Bottom: Loupe Images, ph Andrew Wood/Mikko Puotila's apartment in Espoo, Finland. Interior design by Ulla Koskine (www.woodnotes.fi). 116 Top: Reflexstock/Radius Images. Bottom: Reflexstock/ Naturbild RF/Anders Haglund. 117 Top: Reflexstock/NFZ/Ka Ho Leung. Bottom: Reflexstock/Imagebroker. 118 Top: Loupe Images. Bottom: Reflexstock/NFZ/Sergey Oganesov. 119 Top: Reflexstock/NFZ/Ivanov Arkady. Left: Reflexstock/ NFZ/Sally Wallis. Right: Reflexstock/Imagebroker. Bottom: Reflexstock/ heritage/The Museum of East Asian Art/ Heritage-Images.120 Top: Reflexstock/ Westend61/Achim Sass. Bottom: Getty Images/ Ferdinand Daniel. 122 Reflexstock/Stock Connection/Novastock. 123 Top: Reflexstock/ Westend61/Creativ Studio Heinemann. Middle: Reflexstock/Radius Images. Bottom left: Reflexstock/Westend61/Gaby Wojciech. Bottom right: Reflexstock/Westend61/ Creativ Studio Heinemann. 124 Top: Loupe Images. Bottom: Reflexstock/ Imagebroker. 125 Top: Loupe Images, ph Caroline Arber/Rosanna Dickinson. Bottom: Reflexstock/ Yali Shi. 127 Top left: Reflexstock/ First Light/Olivier Mackay. 128 Top: Getty Images/Tom Grill. Bottom: Getty Images. 129 Top left: Reflexstock/ Stocktrek Images. Top right: Getty Images/Medioimages/ Photodisc. 131 Reflexstock/ NFZ/Jelena Zaric. 132 Top: Getty Images/Image Source. Bottom: Reflexstock/Robert Harding/ Fraser Hall. 133 Top: Reflexstock/NFZ/Alvin Teo. Bottom: Reflexstock/ Panthermedia Basic/Kai Krüger. 134 Loupe Images, ph Claire Richardson/Marianne Cotterill's house in London. 135 Reflexstock/NFZ/ Kheng Guan Toh. 138 Getty Images.139 Reflexstock/Uppercut RF/Heather Monahan Photography. 140 Reflexstock/Fancy /Tammy Hanratty. 141 Reflexstock/Panthermedia Basic/Vangelis Thomaidis. 142 Loupe Images. 143 Top: Reflexstock/CulturaRF/Philip Lee Harvey. Bottom: Reflexstock/NFZ/Marcus Miranda.144 Left: Reflexstock/NFZ/Mariano Ruiz. Right: Reflexstock/ DAJ. 145 Bottom: Reflexstock/ Tetra/Klaus Tiedge.146 Right: Reflexstock/Fancy. Bottom left: Reflexstock/Fancy. 147 Top: Loupe Images/Chris Everard. Bottom: Reflexstock /Designpics.148 Top: Getty Images/Image Source. Bottom: Reflexstock/NFZ /Cathy Yeulet. 149 Bottom: Reflexstock/Fancy. 151 Top: Reflexstock/ BlendRF/ ERproductions Ltd. 153 Top: Reflexstock/Chris Cole. Bottom: Reflexstock/ Corbis.154 Top: Reflexstock/Corbis. Bottom: Reflexstock/ Westend61/ Andreas Koschate. 155 Top: Reflexstock/Corbis. Bottom: Reflexstock/OJO Images/Chris Ryan. 156 Reflexstock/Radius Images.

Front cover: Getty (above right). Back cover: Photolibrary (center); Getty (below left and right). Quilted numbers, Louise Bell: 14, 16, 17, 18, 19, 20, 21, 22, 23, 24, 25, and 149. Illustration, Stephen Dew: 60, 64, 65, 68, 69, 70, 71, 74, 75, 78, 87, 94, 105, 109, 127, 129, 130, 134, 135.